4-H GUIDE
TO DOG TRAINING AND DOG TRICKS

Tammie Rogers

Voyageur Press

A portion of the sales of this product will be used to promote 4-H educational programs. No endorsement of this product by 4-H is implied or intended. Use of the 4-H Name & Emblem is authorized by USDA.

4-H is a community of six million young people across America learning leadership, citizenship, and life skills. National 4-H Council is the private sector, nonprofit partner of National 4-H Headquarters (USDA). The 4-H programs are implemented by the 106 Land-Grant Universities and the Cooperative Extension System through their 3,100 local Extension offices across the country. Learn more about 4-H at www.4-H.org. 18 USC 707

First published in 2009 by Voyageur Press, an imprint of MBI Publishing Company, 400 First Avenue North, Suite 300, Minneapolis, MN 55401 USA

Voyageur Press titles are also available at discounts in bulk quantity for industrial or sales-promotional use. For details write to Special Sales Manager at MBI Publishing Company, 400 First Avenue North, Suite 300, Minneapolis, MN 55401 USA.

To find out more about our books, visit us online at www.voyageurpress.com.

Library of Congress Cataloging-in-Publication Data

Rogers, Tammie.
4-H guide to dog training and dog tricks / Tammie Rogers.
        p. cm.
Includes index.
ISBN 978-0-7603-3629-8 (flexibound)
1. Dogs—Training. I. Title. II. Title: Guide to dog training and dog tricks.
SF431.R615 2009
636.7'0887—dc22

                                    2009017040

ISBN-13: 978-0-7603-3629-8

Edited by Amy Glaser
Design Manager: Katie Sonmor
Layout by Pauline Molinari
Cover Design by the Book Designers
Front cover image: Juniors Bildarchiv/Photolibrary

All photography by Robert Rogers

Book reviewed by:
Barbara A. Taylor
4-H volunteer Washington State University Extension, Pierce County.

Printed in China

CONTENTS

Dedication

This book is dedicated to my parents, John and Carol, without whose love and support I could not have become the independent-thinking, creative person I am today.

And to my husband, Robert, whose strength and commitment to me and my dreams have been inspiring beyond comprehension, thank you. You are truly the wind beneath my wings.

Acknowledgments

I am sincerely grateful to the following individuals for their assistance, which was offered in so many different ways.

Almost nothing I do would be possible without the support of my husband, Robert. He has been a rock and was most understanding as the deadline for this book approached. I love you.

Pam Vollmer, for whom I trained a service dog named Paden, has taught me so many things as I have watched her on her journey over the past several years to become an increasingly capable dog handler. Most recently, her assistance reviewing the manuscript was so helpful. I truly cherish her caring and compassionate kindness and willingness to help in so many little ways.

Marty Block, my good friend, confidant, and fellow dog lover, has been my sounding board for more years than I can count. I appreciate her perspective and her loyalty more than she probably knows.

As students, Lisette Ehret and her beautiful collie Adair have been an instructor's dream. It was with the greatest pleasure that I watched Lisette become an autonomous, highly competent dog handler who should be proud of her accomplishments.

I'd like to thank Carla Zolman for her legal expertise.

Thanks to Carla Zolman, Pandora Ray, and Jo Ellen Alsop for their assistance with the manuscript review.

The many 4-H members who have participated in my fair prep classes have been influential in my journey toward writing this book. I thank you and your dedicated parents. The 4-H members and their dogs who modeled for many of the photos in this book are:

- Trishia Buzzard and Caroline (While no photos of them are included due to a lighting issue on the day they modeled, I still appreciate their time.)
- Kayleigh Magnus and Snowbelle
- Sara Milburn and Shania
- Caleb Moody and Dusty
- Faith Mooreland and James
- Derek Niemeyer and Rocky
- Sydney Rosborough and Sadie
- Thank you Jane Schipma and border collie, Ace. I am so proud of your accomplishments together, and I appreciate that you posed for photos in this book.

And I would like to thank Amy Glaser, acquisitions editor at Voyageur Press, for asking me to author this book. I truly appreciate the opportunity to share my thoughts on dog training via this medium.

INTRODUCTION

It was 1986. I was a couple years out of college and living in an apartment in Chicago. I had acquired two dogs by that time: a mutt I called Macho and a purebred Labrador retriever I named Stella. At a training club near my home, I had moved Macho through the intermediate level of competitive trialing. He was doing well at "fun matches"—informal events intended to provide practice for real shows. Then I discovered that as a mixed breed, he was not allowed at the official American Kennel Club (AKC) trials. With newfound education on dog training and management, I acquired Stella from a quality breeder. She was just a pup when my parents came to visit that spring day in 1986.

While I attempted to demonstrate to my parents how well I was doing on my own, I had failed to explain my plans to Stella. During the visit, the yellow Lab did all the things that puppies do. She jumped up on my mother, knocking from her hands the gifts she had brought to me. She side-swiped my father as he approached a chair, nearly knocking him over. She pranced off to my bedroom and promenaded back into the front room proudly carrying a pair of my underwear that she pulled out of a laundry basket.

I addressed each infraction to the best of my ability, using the information I had learned at dog school. Good timing, appropriate feedback, proper attitude, and presence were all part of the communication. Controlling my own frustration, remaining calm, and dispensing clear consequences for Stella's behavior were also part of the equation. After watching my interactions with Stella, my father, a man who I considered quick to give his opinion even at the risk of hurting my feelings, spoke. "You will be a very good parent one day." Coming from him, I considered it a supreme compliment. That was years ago, but I still remember it as if it were just yesterday.

Training a dog is very much like parenting a child. However, we cannot forget that our pet dogs are not human. We must take expertise that we develop in our relationships with humans and merge it with knowledge about this unique species with which we share our lives. Dogs neither are wild animals nor are they furry children. They are a species developed by man, quite often in man's image. So unique they are, and so similar they are to us, and yet, so different too.

With knowledge and understanding, just about anyone can train his or her own dog. But my experience teaching 4-H members helped me to recognize that, at times, it can be better to be young and impressionable, rather than hardened and set in your ways.

There is a special bond between kids and dogs. To honor that relationship, the 4-H program offers children and young adults the opportunity to demonstrate the fruits of their labors at sanctioned county fairs. By attending weekly classes, these youngsters have learned about basic dog care. They have received instruction on proper training and proficient handling. In doing so, they have developed a strong bond and indeed a true friendship with their dogs. Members who compete in the 4-H dog program learn about the importance of guardianship—an activity that requires love, attention, and sound leadership. Dogs of all shapes and dispositions are able to learn the required skills to compete with their handlers at 4-H competitions.

Shutterstock

Developing mutual respect is of paramount importance during training. When the appropriate methods are applied, a dog blossoms into a truly dedicated partner and the handler gains confidence and trust in his or her dog. When competing at an obedience trial, the relationship is evident. Some dogs even smile back at their owners.

When it comes to communicating with their dogs, I think children have one up on adults. I speculate that because dogs are rather like kids, who require boundaries set for their behavior, rules to follow, and clear-cut instruction, children are more in tune with what their dogs need. Kids are living in that moment, themselves.

On the other hand, adults can tap into talents they have developed while raising their own children, supervising employees, or developing and growing a healthy connection with a partner or spouse. Teaching a dog is a way to develop a comfortable and rewarding relationship. It is also a means of learning how to appropriately impose one's will upon another being to create trust, develop loyalty, maintain respect, and gain proper authority— without losing the need to have some fun along the way.

This book is designed to introduce methods that are useful to train the common obedience commands, including those exhibited at 4-H fair competitions and AKC obedience trials. It will also explain how to teach your dog a variety of useful tasks and fun tricks.

Gina Smith/Shutterstock

Parts of a Dog

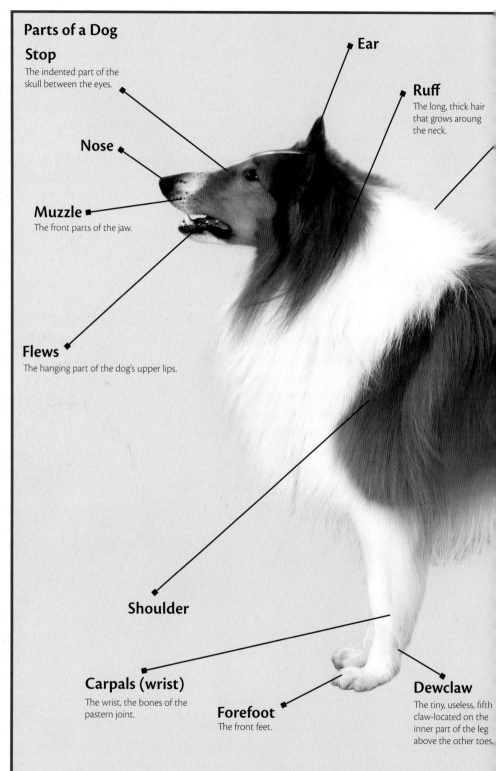

Stop
The indented part of the skull between the eyes.

Ear

Ruff
The long, thick hair that grows around the neck.

Nose

Muzzle
The front parts of the jaw.

Flews
The hanging part of the dog's upper lips.

Shoulder

Carpals (wrist)
The wrist, the bones of the pastern joint.

Forefoot
The front feet.

Dewclaw
The tiny, useless, fifth claw-located on the inner part of the leg above the other toes.

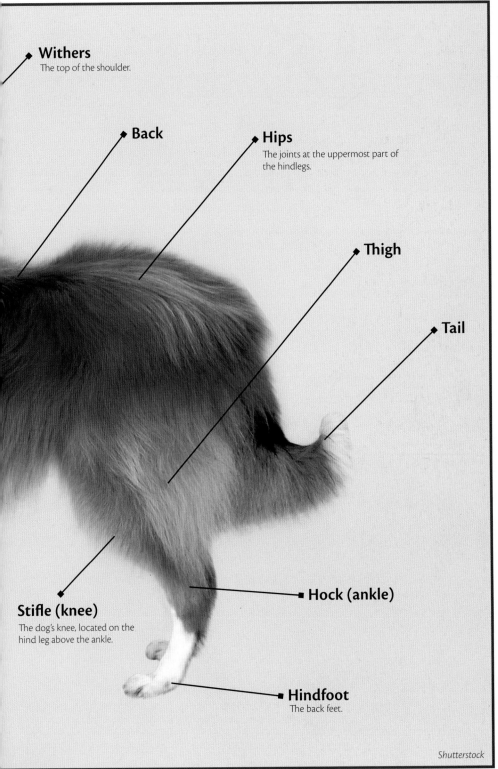

Withers
The top of the shoulder.

Back

Hips
The joints at the uppermost part of
the hindlegs.

Thigh

Tail

Stifle (knee)
The dog's knee, located on the
hind leg above the ankle.

Hock (ankle)

Hindfoot
The back feet.

TRAINING METHODS

There are three different methods that can be used to teach your dog just about any task, trick, or obedience exercise you can imagine. The first two methods are quite different from each other, both in methodology and in the way the dog perceives the information coming from the trainer. The third method is a way of melding the two basic processes to provide highly reliable behavior.

This tiny, seven-day-old border collie puppy has the promise to develop into an extraordinary animal. It could become a herding champion, a search and rescue dog, an agility competitor, or a dedicated service dog for a disabled individual. However, without proper early socialization and exceptional management, it will not reach its true potential. Its future owner must be dedicated to providing boundaries for proper behavior and enriching activities to stimulate its mind and body. *Heidi Brand/Shutterstock*

The Social Compliance Method is designed to:

- Eliminate unwanted behaviors
- Tap into a dog's natural desire to be accepted as a social member of a pack
- Set standards for typical manners or general good conduct

The Incentive Method is designed to:

- Create desired behaviors
- Build on a dog's natural desire to gain assets
- Lure a dog into performing behaviors
- Pair rewards with desired behaviors (lured or naturally occurring)
- Help a dog perform complex, multidimensional tasks

The Comprehensive Method is designed to:

- Establish clear boundaries around behaviors
- Set a high standard of performance for tasks that were taught using the Incentive Method
- Address issues such as distraction or substandard performance, most specifically for exercises taught by the Incentive Method

Tasks such as retrieving a dumbbell are easy to teach to a dog, especially one that wants to please his owner. This ten-month-old border collie has learned to fetch and hold a dumbbell. His breed, one that has been designed to partner with people to perform a job, contributed to how quickly he learned. However, if he didn't have proper care as a youngster, his training would have been far less speedy. Dogs are pack animals. They need to be part of the family to reach their true potential.

The Social Compliance Method

This method is designed to eliminate bad behaviors. It is a correction-based method. The basic steps in this method are:

- Proactively identify the precursor behaviors leading to unwanted behaviors. This could be something like a dog dropping his head or shoulders just before he jumps up.
- Provide a warning signal. This is typically a spoken word or phrase, but it can be a visual signal.
- If the dog does not heed the warning and cease the bad behavior, correct the dog.

When using this method, it is important to avoid being emotional when reprimanding a dog. Make certain that the correction is above the threshold needed to change the behavior. Avoid nagging.

The greatest benefit of this method is that, if done properly, it can stop the dog's unwanted behavior permanently or for a very long time. Another advantage is that it emulates the natural method in which dogs inform each other about acceptable, social behavior.

Dogs communicate with each other by setting boundaries and enforcing those limits. Dogs often establish a pack hierarchy, and the individuals that are higher in the society set limits for others in the family structure. A socially balanced, senior dog warns another dog that it is about to penetrate a boundary, such as: "Do not come closer to my food

At just eight weeks old, this border collie has already developed a strong desire to seek the attention and affection of humans. Hearing a door open signals them that their caregiver is about to arrive. Such focused attention at such a young age is remarkable. A result of several thousand years of domestication and artificial selection, the affinity to humans that dogs present is extraordinary. Developed from wild, social canines, our dogs ache to be integrated members of our society.
Andrii Muzyka/Shutterstock

bowl." This is often done by baring the teeth, lowering the head, or other body posturing like pinning back the ears. If that signal is not sufficient, the dog may add a growl. If the intruding dog does not heed these two warnings (visual and auditory), then the senior dog backs up the warning with a quick nip or bite, usually around the face or neck.

The physical correction is sufficient to make the junior dog back down without additional squabbling. However, the nip is rarely damaging (no blood is drawn), and there is no fighting—just clear communication. Dogs are very accustomed to getting information through this process of visual and/or auditory warnings backed up with physical correction. In order to set the borders for our dogs, we use the same method of first providing a warning, then backing it up with a very meaningful, quick and to-the-point correction. Using a training collar that can deliver this sort of message takes advantage of a good tool as well as provides consistent, fair correction.

For any behavior, there is a threshold for change. If we correct the dog above the threshold, the unwanted behavior ends. If we do not influence the dog above the threshold, we simply nag the dog. When using a correction-based method, it is imperative that we truly correct the dog. Dogs do not nag each other. They are effective and efficient at communicating when a behavior is not tolerated. Emulating this process is an important goal in the Social Compliance Method.

While mimicking the natural canine method of communication sounds like a great idea, we humans lack a long muzzle full of powerful teeth. Our faces are flat. We do not grimace well. Few of us can pin back our ears. We are bipedal, which places our faces well above the dog's line of sight. For that reason, baring our teeth as a warning signal is not terribly effective. With the Social Compliance Method, we replace growling and grimacing with words and phrases as warning signals.

We are also unable to snap at or hold down a dog in our jaws the way that senior pack members do to offending lower ranking individuals. Therefore, we will use a collar to provide the physical correction and use a leash to gain access to the collar. It is important that the dog knows from whom the correction is coming. Using our own voices and our own touch (via the lead and collar) helps the dog understand that we are the one delivering the reprimand for an unwanted behavior. If the dog is not wearing a collar or lead when he presents an offending act, we can still correct him. We can use our hands (with stiffened fingers) and poke at the dog's neck or cheek to emulate the required "bite."

Corrections should not have emotional tags associated with them. Corrections should not be paired with anger, disappointment, or frustration. Corrections are merely well-timed information that let the dog know that his behavior (or the behavior he is about to present) is unacceptable and should not be repeated. If you sense you are getting angry when correcting the dog, purge those negative feelings before continuing the training session. If necessary, walk away.

It is important to let the dog know, very clearly, that when you say a command (such as "sit"), you expect him to do so without any hesitation. This is a fair way of teaching a dog. Allowing the dog to disobey *sometimes* because you are not prepared to follow through

Threshold to Change Behavior

Truly Correct = Changed Behavior

Nagging = Continued Bad Behavior

on your expectations makes them less clear for the dog. Unclear expectations may result in frustration. Frustration may lead to acting out. When a dog acts out, you may feel a need to correct him. In reality, it may be because you were not consistent with your training and expectations that the dog was naughty. Always be prepared to back up your command before you utter the command word.

Potential Pitfalls of the Social Compliance Method

The challenge that some owners encounter with the Social Compliance Method is that they do not pay enough attention to the dog's behavior. This results in their losing the opportunity to correct the dog for thinking about doing the undesired action. Once a dog is actually in the act of the unwanted behavior, it is far more difficult to correct it. A dog that is about to nip is easier to effectively correct than a dog that is in the act of nipping. Correcting after the nip happens is fairly ineffective.

The Incentive Method

This method is designed to create desired behaviors. Most people who have owned a dog have some experience using the Incentive Method to teach their pet. All animals move toward experiences that they find pleasurable, especially those things that are important for survival, such as acquiring food. Teaching a puppy to sit is easy to do. It is a simple series of steps that many people tend to figure out on their own.

1. Hold a treat in front of the puppy's nose.
2. Move it slowly upward toward the ceiling.
3. Use command words, such as "Ginger, sit."
4. Watch the pup's nose go up and the rump go down.
5. Deliver the treat as soon as the puppy sits.
6. Voila! The puppy soon learns to sit for the treat.

Potential Pitfalls of the Incentive Method

Unfortunately, many people report that, without the treat, the dog doesn't behave as expected. This is not because using the Incentive Method always results in unreliable behavior. But that is a potential downfall if incentive training isn't implemented properly. Timing the delivery of the treat and deciding when to reduce or eliminate the treats have a bearing on how reliable the results will be.

Luring

Using a treat to teach a puppy to sit is an example of luring. Luring a dog with a treat and then rewarding him is one of the easiest exercises for most folks to understand and execute. Some drawbacks of luring include:

- The dog may become reliant on the physical gesture rather than learning the English word/command.
- The dog may become reliant on receiving the treat and may not perform without the bribe.
- The handler may not be able to manipulate the treat into all the required positions to "lure" the dog towards the behavior.
- The handler may not properly time the elimination of both the gesturing and the delivery of the treat, which is critical.

Using food to reward a dog's behavior is called positive reinforcement. It is one of four learning processes defined by psychologist B. F. Skinner. Animals learn in a variety of ways, and positive reinforcement is a strong motivator. It can direct a dog toward actions that the handler finds acceptable. However, it is far less effective at stopping unwanted behaviors.

Targeting

Another way to help the dog move towards presenting the desired behavior is through a process called targeting. With targeting, the dog is trained, first, to have an affinity to follow or touch an object. The object can be your hand, a pencil, the lid of a yogurt container, a telescoping pointer stick, or any other article. Once the dog knows the touch or target command, he can be lured to move by following the target. Some people argue that teaching a dog to follow a target in order to lure the dog into the desired position will keep him more focused on performing the task. In contrast, using the actual food lure to get the dog to move into the desired position keeps the pups focused on the food instead.

Reducing and Eliminating the Reward

In the end, it is important how and when the food is removed from the picture. Nobody wants to be forever reliant on food to get their dog to perform. Regardless of how you choose to get the dog to carry out the behavior, once he is able to do the task fairly reliably (say around 80 percent of the time) it is prudent to begin reducing the food or toy reward. In the beginning, do not completely stop offering the food, but instead, slowly introduce times when the dog only receives verbal praise, rather than the treat. Do so in a random fashion so that the dog does not learn to predict when the treat may or may not be delivered.

Break It Down

Along with directly luring the dog to perform the task and teaching him to target to an object in order to better guide him towards the end behavior, it can be important to break down the expected trick into smaller parts. For example, a recall exercise at an obedience trial may include the following components:

- The dog must assume a sit position on command.
- The dog must stay when told while the handler walks 30 feet away. The dog should not get up, sniff around, or otherwise be distracted.
- The dog should quickly and directly return to the handler when called.
- The dog should sit directly in front of the handler and close enough that the handler can touch the dog's head. He must not sniff or otherwise move until instructed to do so.
- When commanded, but not before, the dog should assume the proper heel position by walking around and behind the handler or by swinging around to the left of the handler. The dog should sit straight and square.

Many of the components of the recall exercise can be taught using the Incentive Method. But, clearly, if one were to wait to deliver a treat until the dog had performed all of the components of the final exercise, many dogs would fail to learn the expectations. Breaking down the final version of the skill into smaller pieces and rewarding each smaller component is important. For example, teaching the dog to sit squarely in front of the handler can be accomplished without first calling the dog.

The benefit of using an incentive-based method is that, so long as the dog wants the incentive (food treat), most dogs will attempt to perform some action to acquire the treat. This, however, can be a downfall as well. When a dog believes there is a reward coming, he may attempt to experiment to acquire the reward. This is especially true when he has already successfully learned a series of tasks for which he has been compensated. Some experimental behaviors are undesirable. For example, a dog may attempt to jump up to get the reward that we are using to help him learn to sit or shake paw.

Experimenting, however, can also be a very good thing. If we want the dog to figure out how to accomplish a task that we struggle with using a direct luring or targeting approach, some dogs will try to earn the incentive through creative testing. If, at those times, the dog does perform a behavior that can be very useful, the handler can reward the behavior and turn it into a new task.

Another downfall of the incentive/positive reinforcement method is that the decision about whether or not to comply with a command or expectation is left up to the dog and how much he is driven to acquire the reward. Working for incentives does not require respect or reverence for a leader or authority figure. Working for food incentives is not based on compliance. Dogs do not utilize the Incentive Method to develop and uphold societal norms of behavior with each other.

When using the Incentive Method, begin practicing in an environment that has very few distractions. In particular, since you will be using food rewards, do not work where other pets can disrupt your training session. The Incentive Method offers no consequence when the dog chooses to no longer participate in the training. This is why it can seem to be a very unreliable method and why, for many of the tasks, the Comprehensive Method is recommended as a final stage in the dog's training.

The value of the food reward is also important for success with the Incentive Method. A high-value reward is one that the dog finds particularly satisfying and therefore will work harder to gain. Fresh meats, cheeses, and super premium treats are often in this category. Lower-value treats might include the dog's daily dry kibble. When a task is difficult, it can be beneficial to use a reward

with higher value. Teaching a dog to do something physically challenging, such as climbing a ladder, may require real, roasted chicken or beef. Contrary to what might seem logical, when teaching some of the more mentally complex tasks, you should actually use a lower-value treat. This allows the dog the chance to experiment or focus on the new behavior rather than be overly stimulated with the acquisition of the treat.

Using a Bridge

There are many tasks or behaviors that would be nearly impossible to teach without the use of incentives. While the Social Compliance Method works at the dog's basic need to be socially accepted, teaching a dog tricks that have no inherent significance for survival falls far outside a dog's natural drive to perform. Therefore, as his teacher, you need to quickly identify for your dog that a specific behavior is what you want. Giving him food immediately after he presents the task is a perfect way to do that.

There are times, however, when it's difficult to deliver the food reward immediately after the dog performs the new trick. In those instances, it is helpful to let him know you are happy with what he has done and to deliver a treat shortly thereafter. Unfortunately, if you wait to deliver the treat, you may reward the wrong behavior.

For more complicated tasks, there is a method that will help your dog understand that you are pleased with what he has just done, even if you cannot get the food to him right away. It is an offshoot of the early observation that Ivan Pavlov, the Russian scientist, noted. If he rang a bell prior to feeding the dogs, they would begin to salivate upon hearing the bell. The sound of the bell became synonymous with food, resulting in salivation prior to the dog actually receiving the meal. If you condition your dog to a sound by pairing it with the actual food reward, you can let the dog know exactly when he performs the exercise that you are pleased. Then, you can deliver the treat a few seconds later, and the dog still understands that it was the behavior that you identified with your special sound that you are rewarding. Why? It is because the sound has become synonymous with the pleasant sensation of receiving food.

Some trainers use a small clicking device to pair clicks with their food rewards. Others simply use a very specific word. The term "bridge" is used to describe the sound, since it bridges the gap between alerting the dog that he is correct and the delivery of the treat. What is important is that the dog knows that the sound is the same as the reward. Before you do any training, you may want to teach the dog the meaning of your bridge.

Making the association is as simple as presenting the sound and giving a treat instantly, without delay. If this is done for twenty to a hundred times, the dog's brain will pair the sound or word with the reward and the bridge will elicit the same response in the dog as receiving food, which, for most animals, is the feeling of satisfaction.

Although many people prefer using a clicker as a bridge, it can be a challenge to add the clicking device into the equation when teaching a sophisticated trick, such as retrieving. Throwing and receiving an object, delivering a treat, and working a clicker at the same time can be overwhelming. Using a word like "yes," "good," or "right" as a bridge reduces the stress on the handler, since she will always have her voice with her. But dogs are very perceptive to our emotional status. When making the pairing of a special word and a treat, remain calm and unemotional.

The Comprehensive Method

The great value of the Incentive Method is that we can explain what we would like our dog to do even if it makes little or no sense to her. While training a dog to respect a barrier, refrain from chasing the cat, or to stay in one spot is easy to do with the Social Compliance Method, it would be wholly unacceptable to teach a dog to, say, negotiate a complicated obstacle using a correction-based method. Creating desired behaviors is best accomplished via a method that encourages the dog to try and by rewarding his efforts,

Pitfalls to Avoid When Creating the Association between the Bridge and the Reward

- Since dogs are more tuned into body language than spoken words, avoid moving your body—and most importantly the hand with which you deliver the treat—until after the sound is delivered.
- If your dog is not "present" for the training, as in he is distracted by something like a cat coming into the room or the doorbell ringing, he is less apt to learn the significance of your association. Work in a distraction-free environment.
- Refrain from adding emotion to the special word. The reason that some trainers prefer a clicking device is to avoid this possibility.

no matter how simple they may be in the beginning. We correct unwanted behavior, but we must reward desired actions.

Unfortunately, the Incentive Method leaves the choice of whether or not to perform a task in the paws of the dog. The dog will determine if, when, and for how long she will do the behavior. If the task is a trick that you want to show to your friends, that might not be so bad. But to establish reliability, we need to let the dog know our expectations. The Incentive Method offers no options when a dog chooses to no longer participate in training. This is why for many tasks, the Comprehensive Method is recommended.

There is typically only one county fair each year, and there is only one dog show at that fair. A 4-H-er who hopes to qualify for the state fair dog competition needs to do his or her very best at the county level. At an obedience trial, a dog that lies down during the one-minute sit-stay exercise or refuses to come when called on the first command will receive a zero for that skill and will not earn a qualifying score. The handler cannot take food into the obedience ring. To do well, the dog must perform at a high standard without the lure of a food treat.

The Comprehensive Method helps the dog learn that behaviors he learned though the Incentive Method will be expected. Corrections will not be used to create behaviors, but they can be implemented when the dog chooses to refuse or is distracted and

These dogs were trained to sit by their 4-H handlers. But why do they stay put? Why don't they choose to visit with the other dogs in the lineup? The Comprehensive Method takes skills taught using the Incentive Method and helps dogs conform to their owners' standards and expectations. The dogs are attentive to their handlers. The handlers are calm and relaxed in the knowledge that their dogs understand the expectations of the exercise.

fails to complete a command. Moving from the purely Incentive Method to the correction method is easy and natural. Once the dog understands the meaning behind a word and is performing the command consistently, there may still be times when he decides to ignore our expectations. When, for example, the dog gets up from a sit without permission, he is presenting an unwanted behavior. The Social Compliance Method can be applied to set the expectations for the behavior.

It is best to correct the dog for *thinking* about getting up. Paying attention to the dog's behavior and providing a verbal warning, then a correction if the dog does not stay in place, is highly effective at setting the standard you expect. Catching the dog before he actually gets out of the sit position also means that the correction does not have to be very severe. A simple collar check is often all that is necessary if the handler is proactive.

An owner who has high aspirations for her dog's behavior and is capable of upholding them *consistently* will create a very happy dog. Dogs by nature are able and willing to maintain a high level of compliance to societal rules. A lazy owner creates an unhappy dog. Dogs do not respect an inconsistent leader. A dog that cannot respect his leader is not content because he is left in the position of aching for stronger leadership. Some dogs fill the void by taking control of situations, sometimes by force. Other dogs retreat and become shy or skittish in those same stressful situations.

We owe it to our dogs to provide clear information about our expectations and to reinforce the standards that we set on a highly consistent basis. After we teach a dog a behavior, perhaps using the Incentive Method, we can transfer the meaning of that skill from one where the dog is seeking food to one where the dog is seeking approval as a social, compliant, respectful working partner.

Avoiding Potential Pitfalls of the Comprehensive Method

- Do not implement corrections around an incentive-created behavior until the dog is performing the behavior reliably around 80 percent of the time.
- Do not implement corrections around an incentive-created behavior before beginning phase out of the rewards.
- Correct the unwanted behaviors that exist around an incentive-created behavior, not the actual behavior. These would include becoming distracted or refusal.
- Example: A dog that is performing the task of retrieving an article around 95 percent reliably (that no longer requires rewards for each retrieve) gets distracted by the doorbell ringing and refuses to retrieve. The dog should receive a correction for becoming distracted to establish expectations about remaining on task. However, a correction should not be used to make the dog retrieve since the dog did not learn to retrieve through corrections.

THE TOOLS

The Lead

The most basic tools required for training a dog are a collar and a lead. The lead is simply used to gain access to the dog, but it must never apply tension to the dog's neck, nor should it be used as a restraining device. Regardless of the method employed to train your dog, there is rarely a need to hold back, tie up, or otherwise restrict a dog during training. The dog should be self-restrained. If it is not, then the Social Compliance Method should be used to teach the dog proper etiquette and manners.

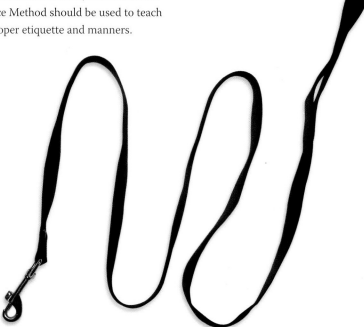

Nylon or leather leashes are recommended for basic training.

Since the lead is not required to restrict the dog, it does not need to be big and strong. An inexpensive nylon web leash that can be purchased at a discount store is sufficient for most applications. However, some people prefer the feel of leather. If so, there are many leather leads from which to choose of various widths and styles, including flat and braided.

Regardless of whether a nylon web or a leather lead is chosen, it need not be wide and bulky, even for larger dogs. Choose the lead that fits best into your hands and can be easily folded in an accordion pleat within your fist for when the full length is not required.

A metal chain leash is not acceptable for a couple of reasons. First, it is very difficult to double up into the palm of your hand. Holding a metal chain can be quite uncomfortable for the trainer. Second, its weight can cause the chain to slap the dog in the head, which is an unpleasant experience we should avoid.

Retractable leads are also a bad choice for most training situations. If, when the dog is at a distance, they are dropped, the hard plastic casing can fly across the floor at breakneck speed and injure your dog. The thin cord can quickly wrap around a person's ankle or calf and cause serious damage. The level of control a handler has over the dog on a retractable lead is usually not sufficient for most training applications.

The task or trick will help define the required length of the lead for any given exercise. For the most common exercises, a 5- to 6-foot leash is sufficient. For 4-H or AKC obedience competitions, a 6-foot lead is typically recommended in classes where the lead is used during the class.

Tools for the Incentive Method

Since the Incentive Method is based on the dog's desire to work towards attaining a reward, the selection of the incentive is essential. Some dogs will work to gain access to a very special toy. If this is the case, restrict your dog's access to that toy to only during training times. It will make it a more valuable reward.

Most people choose to use food for incentive training. This is often paired with a bridge, which can be a clicking device. If you choose to use a clicker, there are many models from which you can choose. Pick one that fits well in your hand. If you are working on tasks, such as retrieving, that require the use of both

---

Since the purpose of the lead is to gain access to the collar, for some situations you may prefer to employ a "tab," or very short lead. For example, when teaching your dog to keep her head out of the open refrigerator door, you may want to give a quick collar correction, but you may not want her to be dragging a full-size lead around the house. Attaching a 3- to 5-inch piece of rope to her collar may be all that is required.

When Using Food as an Incentive

- Use the smallest pieces possible to still incite your dog's enthusiasm.
- Use soft, moist-type treats to reduce crumbs and chewing time.
- Identify several types of treats that cover the range of keenness from your dog so that you can reserve the treat with the highest value to teach the most challenging tasks and still have a treat that will suffice for the less strenuous training times.

your hands, there are clickers that come with a wrist strap.

Your voice may be one of the most important tools you have when training with incentives. While the purists who work exclusively with this method will suggest that using your voice as the bridge requires that your tone remains exactly the same, at all times, it's difficult for most humans to hold back our excitement when our dog performs a new task for the first time. The jubilation that can be heard in our voice at that time does have an influence on our dogs. My experience says that it is a positive influence. Using your voice to share glee and encouragement during training is an important aspect of developing a good working relationship with your dog.

Collar Selection

While using a purely incentive method to encourage a dog to perform tricks can be accomplished without a collar or lead, if a correction is warranted, we need to do so as efficiently and effectively as possible to avoid nagging. We should strive to apply one good correction and be done with it.

A correction is simply an interaction with the dog that changes his unacceptable behavior. Some dogs may feel corrected and strive to change their actions based solely on the handler's tone of voice. A growl, so to speak, coming from a respected human can be considered a correction. If that is all that is required, then that is all that should be applied. But some dogs require a physical touch to shut down unwanted behavior. This can be accomplished with stiffened, outstretched fingers jabbed at the dog's neck or shoulder in much the same way another dog might take a snap at an offending pup. Other dogs require a more focused or higher level of intensity to alter their behavior. For those situations, it is best to use a collar to deliver an appropriate correction. It should be

a goal to deliver one meaningful correction to alter the dog's unacceptable conduct. Nagging should be avoided.

The placement on the dog's neck is as important as the type of collar that is used. When choosing a collar to assist in training and specifically to deliver a meaningful correction, the collar should sit as high on the dog's neck as possible. It will appear to be touching his ears at the back of his neck. This reduces the dog's capacity to overpower the handler. Where the head goes, the body goes. Once the collar is positioned just below the head and above the neck, it is easier to take charge of even the most willful dogs. It also means that the handler does not have to apply as much force in the physical correction if it is required. When a collar is positioned low on the dog's neck, he has access to the most powerful part of his body: his front end assembly, including his shoulders and front legs. Since the goal of any type of physical correction is to resolve a problem as efficiently and effectively as possible, allowing the dog the capacity to overwhelm the handler simply isn't wise.

There are many types of collars. All of them can be used properly with decent success, and all of them can be used incorrectly with poor execution and potential abuse. It is important to understand the collar's design and function prior to putting it on your dog. Before choosing a tool, the handler should answer the question: What am I attempting to accomplish with the collar?

Since the collar should not be used to restrict the dog, the main purpose of the tool during training is to deliver an efficient and effective correction. Because we want to emulate the way that dogs interact with each other when setting standards for behavior, we need to use a collar that will truly deliver a correction and not nag the dog or be abusive to him.

The Buckle Collar

While your final goal should be to work with your dog either without a collar or with a simple buckle collar, the plain buckle collar is a bad option for many dogs as a training device and during initial training. It tends to slide down low on the dog's neck. It is wide and flat, and if used to impose a physical correction, it only offers a dull thud directly across from where the lead is attached to the collar. This most often results in nagging.

The plain buckle collar is a good place to attach personal contact information. In the event that your dog is lost, the tag can mean the difference between being reunited with your pet and losing him forever. While it is customary to include your dog's name on a tag or name plate, for security reasons, I recommend restricting the information to your phone number and address. Once someone knows your dog's name, your dog may respond to that person as if he or she were his owner, potentially making it a challenge to prove ownership.

The Choke Collar

The slip chain collar has deep roots to the traditional training methods employed almost exclusively before 1980. The intended use of a slip chain collar is to apply a "pop and jerk" action. It is meant to emulate the quick bite or snap that one dog delivers to another. While many people have been successful training dogs with this tool, the pros do not typically outweigh the cons, except when in the hands of a highly experienced handler. The choke collar is nearly impossible to maintain high on the dog's neck. To position the collar around the dog's neck, it must be large enough to go over the dog's head. Since the head is typically larger than the neck, especially the very upper-most part, the collar ends up too large. It frequently slips down around the dog's throat. Its single chain design acts much like a piano wire cutting into the dog's neck and often results in that horrid hacking noise when tension restricts the dog's trachea.

While the choke chain can be challenging as a training device, it offers a level of security in that it will constrict around a dog's neck rather than pull off over his head. It is substandard compared to the prong collar in giving a correction above the threshold needed to change a dog's behavior.

The Head Halter

A quick Internet search on how to employ a dog head halter will result in complete confusion. Some advocates of the device suggest that it is a correction tool used to deliver a "quick pop" or "jerk," while others staunchly oppose its use to apply a correction and suggest that the benefit of the tool is that it is not a correcting collar. Other sources suggest that if used as a correction tool, it can cause serious injury to the dog. Most sources suggest that it is to be used as a restraining device rather than a correction tool.

Since one of the primary goals in correcting a dog is to attempt to emulate the natural ways that dogs interact with each other, and since dogs do not use a method of restraint to impose standards for behavior, I do not consider the head halter an appropriate tool during training. Restraint is not the way to move a dog to the status of self-restraint, which is the goal of my training methods.

Dog head halters are a fairly new invention, but that does not necessarily make them better than traditional collars. Ancient Egyptian images from 3000 to 3500 B.C. suggest that domestic dogs were donning collars thousands of years ago. A collar helps control a dog because it applies pressures to the place where dogs yield to pressure when interacting with each other—around the neck.

A choke chain made of nylon offers a softer touch around the dog's neck, but it lacks any sort of sound associated with constriction. Folks who prefer using metal choke chains to train their dogs often report that they can warn a dog of an impending correction by simply jingling the collar. For that reason, the nylon version may lack some of the correction power of the metal model. However, if it is being used strictly as a security device on an already-trained dog, the nylon collar may be preferred for its gentler appearance.

The Prong Collar

In my experience, the most effective tool for delivering a meaningful correction is the pinch or prong collar. Because of its superior craftsmanship, I have had great success with the imported Herm Sprenger brand. Developed in Germany, it is designed to fit well, remain relatively high on the dog's neck, deliver a true correction, minimize the "piano wire" effect of the choke chain, and offset a mismatched ratio of handler to dog weight or strength. Unfortunately, this collar has a very barbaric appearance. It is actually a humane tool in that it does not remain constricted or tight around the dog's neck and is less likely than both a choke collar and a buckle collar to cause a gasping, choking behavior since it does not apply constriction on the esophagus. This collar must be fitted properly. When fitting it on the dog, it should not be placed directly over the dog's head. It should be opened at any link. Links should be removed in order to fit it as high on the dog's neck as possible. It should be a snug fit.

If the prong collar is used properly, it should not be required after the first few weeks of training. If, instead, it is used as a restraint device and the dog is allowed to pull against it, it will lose its effectiveness. Great care should be taken to avoid that from happening.

The dog should not feel the collar unless the handler is delivering a quick correction that is above the threshold to change the dog's behavior. The lead should always be loose unless it is being used to gain access to the collar to deliver a correction. If the collar is used appropriately and a warning word is given before a correction, the dog will learn to adhere to the handler's verbal commands and will no longer require physical corrections. The dog will be acting in a self-restrained manner.

Many people are so put off by the appearance of this collar that they refuse to consider it. A good dog owner will determine whether a specific training tool is appropriate for his or her own dog. To do so, one must collect evidence. You can place this collar on your forearm and fit it properly so that it will affect you the same way it would affect your dog. You can give yourself a correction and see how it feels.

While it may appear odd to folks who routinely put very loose-fitting collars on their dogs, the appropriate placement for a correction collar is very high on the dog's neck. This position gives the handler leverage over the dog's powerful neck and shoulders. It also requires a less intense and severe correction than a collar fitted low on the dog's neck.

The Martingale

The Martingale is designed like the prong collar but replaces the links with a single strap of nylon web. If fitted snugly, the way that a prong collar is meant to fit, it provides more security than a buckle collar because it will constrict rather than slide off the dog's head. It is an accepted collar at AKC obedience events and is a popular option for folks who concern themselves with the constriction quality of a choke chain. However, if fitted snugly, it is just as likely to constrict around the dog's esophagus as a choke collar. The Martingale can be made of thin nylon cord (popular with the conformation handlers) or very wide webbing. People who find a traditional metal choke chain offensive but want a collar that will constrict rather than slip off the head are often drawn to the models with the wide webbing.

With some dogs in certain situations, a Martingale may be able to provide a meaningful correction. But in a side by side comparison, the prong collar will require less intensity and strength of the handler to deliver the information necessary to alter a dog's unwanted behavior.

The Martingale collar is a good transition tool from a correction collar to a plain buckle collar. If fitted properly, the collar does not allow the dog to pull its head out and escape. It can provide a mild correction for a dog that does not require intense feedback for a serious offense.

BEFORE WE GET STARTED

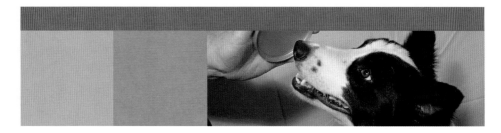

Ensuring success using the various training methods involves a few important steps. First, we need to assess the dog to determine how willing and able it is to accept training. If we determine the dog is not an agreeable participant, we need to address those issues first. Then, to prepare the dog to learn through the various methods, we must take the time to accomplish a few precursor activities.

The Unwilling Student

Before beginning on the adventure of training your pet, it is important to understand a very basic assumption: Antisocial dogs are very difficult, if not impossible, to teach. Prior to jumping into training your dog to do tricks, you may want to employ the Social

Compliance Method to educate your dog about his position in your family structure. Later in training, the method can be used to help set your standard for the tasks you are teaching. What many people refer to as "good manners" are essentially good social skills. Jumping up, invading personal space, failure to relinquish "turf," growling, biting, nipping, charging out of doors, barking, lunging, and chasing cats, bikes, or joggers are all signs of an antisocial dog. These are dogs that do not respect the humans in their world as having rank over them.

As you might imagine, a dog that has no respect for you will probably be somewhat resistant to agree with your wishes. An anti-social dog is like an unruly, stubborn child. It is not very fun to be around this type of dog. The wonderful thing about a domestic dog is that it is a social species. We can use that inherent trait to our advantage when teaching our dogs. A properly social dog is a very happy dog and a willing participant in training. If you find you are struggling to keep your dog's attention during training, it may be because she doesn't care enough to please you. Setting high standards for basic manners can have a big impact on how much your dog wants to work with and for you when learning obedience commands or sophisticated tricks.

Injecting Meaning into the Bridge

Although simply using a piece of food in your hand and luring a dog to perform a behavior can work, conditioning your dog to a bridge word is a superior method at times when you cannot quickly deliver the treat to him. You need to decide whether you will use a word or a device that makes a noise, such as a clicker.

If you plan to train alongside others, consider that your clicker may sound just like your classmate's device, but your voice will be unique, even if you and a classmate use the same bridge word. Some folks like to keep their treats in a "bait bag" they secure around their waist. I choose to put the treats up on a counter close to where I am working. You may use a regular buckle collar and lead to keep him near you so long as he is not struggling against it or pulling away under tension.

To take advantage of the power of classical conditioning, pair a stimulus (such as a specific sound) with a pleasant experience. Here, the handler says "good" and immediately delivers a treat. After a few dozen repetitions, conditioning occurs, and the association between "good" and a treat is forged. Later, the handler can let her dog know he is in proper heel position by uttering her bridge word during the exercise.

To inject meaning into a bridge word or sound:

1. Prepare small-sized morsels of treats that your dog truly enjoys.
2. Take your dog into an area that is free of distractions.
3. Remain as calm and relaxed as possible. Do not move your hand toward the treats prior to presenting the bridge (word or click).
4. Say the bridge word, such as "yes," "good," or "right," or click your clicker.
5. Immediately deliver a treat.
6. Repeat, repeat, and repeat twenty to one hundred times.

Having instilled meaning into the bridge, from this point forward, whenever your dog performs the desired task, you can immediately utter the bridge word (or click your clicker) and the dog will have the physical experience associated with receiving the food even before you deliver it. This will help him understand that you are very pleased with his performance.

Once your dog is performing the task at around 80 percent accuracy, it is time to phase out the reward. Don't do this cold turkey. Rather, set up a schedule to reward around once every three times the dog performs the skills. Then you may reduce that to around every four, then every six times until the dog no longer requires the reward to perform the behavior. Try not to schedule the treats at exact intervals, but switch things up. A dog can learn to expect a treat to be delivered every third time. Reward her with a random pattern that slowly diminishes the delivery of the treat over time.

Touch a Target

When teaching tricks or other skills, it can be valuable to have the power to coerce a dog to move in a certain direction without having to apply any true physical force or without actually moving a treat to the location where you want him to go. Teaching a dog to touch a target is a simple and quick exercise and will result in a dog that is willing to move toward and touch a specific object. The object can be moved where required to assist the dog in knowing what action is expected.

Targets can come in a variety of sizes and shapes. The simplest of all is the palm of your own hand. It is always with you, and once the dog has learned to touch your hand, you can move your hand about and the dog will follow with the intention of touching it. However, I prefer to avoid teaching a dog to target my hand since it can conflict with the idea that the dog should be granted permission to enter a human's personal space and not push into it at will.

A better option is the lid from a cottage cheese or yogurt container, which is typically white, large, and easy to see. Once the dog has learned to touch the plastic lid, it can be attached to an open cabinet door. The dog can be instructed to touch the lid and at the same time often will apply enough force to make the cupboard door swing shut. With practice, your dog can learn to close a cabinet door on command. The target can be tapered by cutting it in half and then half again until the dog no longer requires the image of the target to perform the task of closing the cupboard door with his nose.

A telescoping pointer is also a great target because it can add length to the handler's arm. This is helpful if the handler's body would get in the way of the dog as he attempted to perform the trick or if the handler cannot reach the area where she wants the dog to move. A laser pointer can direct the dog even farther than a telescoping pointer. Care must be taken when teaching dogs to target onto a laser pointer as some dogs can become fixated and obsessed with the moving light.

Here are the steps required to teach a dog to touch a target:

1. Identify a target tool.
2. Stand or sit with your dog facing you.
3. Have your incentives (typically food rewards) ready.
4. Present the target to the dog with an interesting tone to your voice, as if to say, "Look at this wonderful thing!"
5. Hold the target close enough to the dog's face that he can reach out and explore it with his nose (most dogs try to sniff new things) without much movement on his part.
6. Say "touch" or your chosen word for the target.
7. As the dog moves toward the target, say your bridge word and then deliver the treat, making certain that you say the word before moving your hand to give him the reward.
8. Repeat the steps until your dog is actively moving toward the target each time.
9. When he actually touches the target with his nose, make a big deal out of it and give him a few extra treats, so that he realizes that you want him to touch the target.

Once your dog is moving toward the target when you say "touch" most of the time, you can begin to move the target

Target Troubleshooting

If your dog is more focused on getting his food than he is interested in exploring the new object, reduce the value of the food by offering something like his daily kibble rather than a treat that makes him go crazy.

around to encourage him to seek out and touch the target regardless of where it may be. Switch the hand with which you hold the target. Move it farther to one side or the other. Move it far enough away that he has to actually walk to reach it. Each time you make the task more challenging, expect that he may simply sit and look at you as if he doesn't have a clue about what you are expecting of him. At that moment in time, do not lose patience. Stay calm. Do not move. Do not repeat the command to "touch." Give him a bit of time to figure out what you have just asked of him. If he completely loses focus and walks off, you can easily restart the exercise. But if he sits and stares as if perplexed, allow him to think about the problem and solve it. You may be very surprised at how long it takes for your dog to process the new scenario and actually perform the task. But if you are patient at that time, your dog will learn how to learn.

Some of the purists in this training method suggest refraining from uttering the verbal "command" or "cue" word until well after the dog is performing the task. My personal opinion is that while the Incentive Method can be applied to nearly any species of animal with great success, and with most species it may make sense to leave out the "command" until the behavior has become quite reliable, a dog is not just any animal. Dog has been designed by man in man's image for a few thousand years. Dog has the capacity to communicate with humans at a level that is well beyond that in which even tamed wolves express themselves with their human keepers and is light years ahead of the capacity of, say, a wild, captive dolphin's ability to communicate with humans.

Dogs expect us to use human language to converse with them. Like our human counterparts, they gaze in the same direction as do we when we are focused on an

Truman was taught to touch a plastic lid on command. This basic skill forms the basis for a number of tricks and useful tasks. Once a dog learns to touch objects with his nose on command, you can train him to push shut a cabinet door, turn a light switch on or off, or even roll a ball.

Using the Social Compliance Method, you can teach a dog to wait before touching an object. Once a dog learns that he will earn a treat for performing a task, it can be difficult to keep him from doing so at inappropriate times. Setting limits and boundaries for a dog's behavior goes hand in hand with teaching him to perform fun tricks.

important event. They understand us and our emotional essence. They excel best when we communicate thoroughly our expectations because, in fact, they were designed to serve us and work for us.

I recommend using the cue or command word immediately when you initiate a new task. To say "touch" when presenting the target helps the dog because, as humans, we project more when we speak than a mere combination of letters. Dogs read the intentions that we put behind our words. If we are going to take on the role of teacher, then it should be our mission to educate the dog on the meaning behind our words.

Once your dog has mastered touching your initial target, you can train him to touch other objects. If you plan to teach him tricks that will require that he moves about, you may want to use a telescoping target stick for that sort of instruction. But you will find value in teaching him to touch a plastic lid if you want your dog to use his nose to close a cabinet or the door of your laundry dryer, for example. In that case, you can immediately replace the word "touch" with "push" or "close," even though you are asking him to touch it with his nose. Once he transfers the behavior to the plastic lid, you can adhere it to the cabinet with a bit of tape, move it to a position quite close to the lid, tell your dog to "push," and point to the target. Many dogs will quite quickly transfer the behavior from an object in your hand to the target placed on a surface.

Remember to first reward (by saying the bridge word and following up with the treat) approximate behaviors, then expect more accuracy of the behavior over time. If the first time you tape the plastic lid on the cabinet door and say "push," your dog just leans towards it to see what it is, say the bridge word (or click your clicker) and give the treat. Repeat the command word and watch how

your dog moves closer to the target to touch it. Give extra morsels of food and show your excitement for his accomplishment with lots of praise.

Beginning and Ending an Exercise

When we train our dogs it is only fair to provide them some preparatory information before asking them to follow our orders. Prior to most command words you should use the dog's name in a pleasant tone. With that in mind, you should avoid using your dog's name as a means of scolding him. It is disturbingly quite common for folks to shout their dog's name in frustration as he races after a cat or jumps up with excessive exuberance. When used in this manner, the dog's name becomes an ineffective correction. Consequently, the handler is nagging the dog with its own name. Most of us, dogs included, quickly ignore when someone is pestering us. We certainly do not want our dogs to begin to disregard their own names. Take heed to avoid using your dog's name as some sort of ineffective communication when you are angry or frustrated with him.

Choose a word that will signal the end of an exercise. Words like "free," "done," or "okay" are often used. When giving the release word, it is important to avoid excessive excitement in your voice. It is also not an appropriate time to give a reward. You don't want your dog to learn that being off-duty is more exciting than working for you. And you don't want your dog to get overly excited just because he is off task.

Make certain that if you give your dog a command to stay, you also end the exercise. You do not want your dog to finish the exercise for himself because you forgot about him and walked away. Letting the dog know that he is off duty will leave you in control of the commands that you want him to perform.

MANNERS

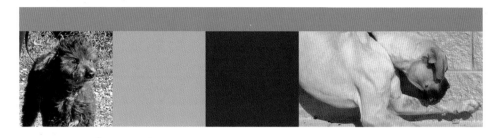

Unlike teaching your dog to do something like "sit" or "down," bad manners are usually actions that we want to remove from our dog's repertoire of behaviors. We will use the Social Compliance Method to do this. It is based on providing clear feedback to the dog that his behavior is undesirable. It taps into the dog's desire to be an accepted member of our pack or family unit.

This image is so common that most people believe it is the only way to walk a dog. Until a dog learns how to follow his leader, most standard training cannot be accomplished. Walking with the right attitude in the proper position is essential for a well-adjusted dog.

Communicating proactively is instrumental in successfully performing the Social Compliance Method. A dog that is just *thinking* about chasing a cat is easier to influence than a dog that is in a full-blown gallop toward the feline. The actual physical intervention needs to be significantly less intense when the dog is in the precursory stage of intention. Intervening early is better for the handler and the dog.

Leash Breaking

Before we can use a lead to access the dog's collar during training, we must teach the dog how to remain respectful on the leash. That means two things. First, the dog must not pull against the lead to move towards an object of his affection, such as food on the floor or a cat he would love to chase. Second, he must not retreat, balk, or rear up in an attempt to escape our influence. The dog must learn that he should remain calmly under the umbrella of our authority.

This is where using a high-quality correction collar, such as the Herm Sprenger prong collar, is valuable. If your dog has been a very strong puller, you will need to refrain from becoming tense, stiffening your arm and hand around the lead, and feeling the need to apply excessive force to counteract his pulling behavior. Remaining calm throughout the exercise is critical.

1. Position the collar high on the dog's neck so that it nearly touches his ears (remove all extra links that would allow it to slip down his neck).
2. Connect a 4- to 6-foot lead to the collar.
3. Remain completely calm and relaxed.
4. As the dog moves toward the end of the lead, allow him to feel the impact of the collar. If he is moving fast toward the end of the lead, stand still and hold the lead firm. This will deliver the appropriate correction for the dog's infraction. If he is moving slowly and gently moves into a pulling behavior on the collar, just as he reaches the end of the lead, give a quick tug of the lead and then immediately release tension.
5. If the collar correction was sufficient, your dog will not pull again in that situation.
6. If the collar correction was insufficient, your dog may attempt to pull again. Repeat the exercise but increase the level of the correction and refrain from a nagging and dragging type of action. Use a very quick, on-then-off-again tug of the collar in an attempt to emulate the rapid and nippy snap that one dog gives to another.
7. Begin to walk very slowly. This can excite the dog to race to the end of the lead again. If he is moving fast toward the end of the lead, stand still and hold the lead firm. It will deliver the appropriate correction for the dog's infraction when he reaches the end. If he is moving slowly and gently moves into a pulling behavior on the collar, give a quick tug of the lead and immediately release tension.
8. Remain very calm and allow the collar to do the work of achieving a successful correction.

I cannot stress enough that the handler's attitude and presence will have a significant bearing on how well the dog responds to a correction. Some dogs will yelp or otherwise protest when they find they are no longer in charge of the direction and speed of travel. Ignoring the objection is critical. To acknowledge it gives the dog the power to use it to his advantage in order to unnerve you.

While dogs can change their behavior upon receiving a single, good correction, most dogs do not immediately generalize our

This is the "before" image of Perry, a poodle-terrier mix that had a cat-chasing problem. It is not uncommon for terriers to focus on small "game," since they were designed to hunt vermin.

How is it that Perry can appear so calm and relaxed in this shot, even in the presence of a cat, when moments before he was charging to catch one? How can the handler control him on a loose lead? The Social Compliance Method emulates the natural communication style that dogs use with each other. Rarely does a dog need to correct an offending dog more than once or twice for the same offense. In the same way, Perry was able to learn in just a few short minutes that pulling, chasing, and lunging after food were unacceptable. When the correction is above the threshold needed to change the behavior, the results are instantaneous.

expectations. A dog can learn not to pull on the lead when in the garage, but once you walk onto the driveway, she may challenge the rule. She may learn to walk properly on lead from the front door to the car door, but may still attempt to race off when you get to the park. Once you set standards for performance in several different scenarios, your dog will begin to generalize your expectations. It is important to practice in a variety of settings at different times and with different levels of distraction to teach your dog that you have a zero tolerance policy for pulling on the lead.

When your dog understands that resisting the lead will no longer be tolerated, it is time to use the same method to actively teach her the meaning of warning words. There is no need to provide any verbal cues about pulling on the lead. It is a behavior that should never be tolerated. We can use the Social Compliance Method to actually teach the dogs the meaning of words that set expectations about limits for behavior.

The natural world is full of warning signals, and an animal brain is designed to pair warning signals with undesirable consequences in order to protect the animal from harm. The black and yellow stripes of a stinging insect are not an attempt at camouflage. Instead, they are designed to provide a specific pattern that can mean a sting is imminent. Once an animal is stung by a bee, the brain pairs up the two signals so that future encounters with bees will elicit a fleeing behavior.

Social animals, like dogs, have developed the capacity to capitalize on this natural reaction in order to maintain social order without requiring that pack members continuously dole out painful punishments for unacceptable behavior. We can tap into that phenomenon to warn dogs that specific behaviors are unwelcome. If we pair a warning word before we deliver a correction for an unwanted behavior, the dog will quickly learn to respect the boundary we are setting.

Wait at the Door

1. Use a correction collar and a lead.
2. Open the door completely.
3. Walk toward the door with the dog but do not allow the leash to tighten into a restraint mode.
4. As you approach the threshold of the door, say the warning word "wait" in a calm, relaxed tone of voice.
5. Continue walking toward the opening (This is an invitation for the dog to proceed even though he was warned).
6. Use the lead to give a very quick, nipping-type collar correction and pull backward toward the dog's tail.

The Social Compliance Method hinges on three very important principles:

1. A warning word must be delivered prior to the dog experiencing a negative consequence.
2. The correction must be above the threshold to change the dog's behavior.
3. A restrained dog will buck your authority, so remember the dog should never feel tension on his neck except for the brief moment it receives a clear, concise collar check correction.

7. As soon as you see the dog's behavior change and he pulls back from the doorway, purge any emotion you may have, say "let's go," and turn from the doorway.

8. Repeat the steps, this time watching carefully to determine whether your dog learned to avoid the open door based on your warning word.

9. As you approach the door, say the warning, "wait," in a calm tone.

10. If the correction was effective, the dog will stop on a loose lead at the threshold of the doorway.

11. A dog that stops should not receive a collar correction. His self-restraint should be rewarded. You may actually be able to see the dog have an "a-ha" moment where he recognizes that your words have meaning and it is worth listening to you.

12. If the dog does not stop at the threshold, you will know that you did not actually correct him the first time. Repeat the exercise, this time decreasing the intensity of your emotion and the tension in your

How Do You Know You Are Doing the Method Properly?

A correction corrects. It resolves the issue. If the dog's behavior does not change, you are nagging him. You are attempting a correction method but missing the mark. What might be contributing to the problem?

Your lack of composure can mask the significance of a physical correction. It is vitally important to remain relaxed when you use a correction-based method. Do not raise your voice. Do not lose your cool. Do not attach emotions to your behavior. Act like a dog. Give prompt, clear feedback without any anger or frustration.

own body and mind, and increasing the impact of the physical correction.

Do Not Jump Up

Using the Social Compliance Method to stop a dog from jumping requires that you follow the same steps as "wait at the door":

1. Use a correction collar and a lead.

2. Have a helper who your dog is likely to jump on approach the dog.

3. Keep the lead loose and remain calm.

4. As your helper approaches, say the warning word "off" in a calm, relaxed tone of voice.

5. As the helper moves into your dog's personal space, look for any signals that she might jump up.

6. If the dog begins to jump, use the lead to give a very quick, nipping-type collar correction downwards towards the ground.

7. As soon as you see the dog's behavior change and she settles back down on all four feet, remain calm and praise her softly.

8. Repeat the steps, this time watching carefully to determine whether your dog learned to avoid jumping up based on your warning word.

9. As your helper approaches again, say the warning "off" in a calm tone.

10. If the correction was effective, the dog will relax and keep all four feet on the ground as the helper comes near you.

11. A dog that relaxes and does not attempt to jump up should not receive the collar correction. Her self-restraint should be rewarded.

12. If the dog chooses to jump up again, you will know that you did not actually correct the dog the first time. Repeat the exercise. This time, decrease the intensity of your emotion and the tension in your own body and mind, and increase the impact of the physical correction.

Jumping up, another common problem, is an antisocial act. Lower-ranking individuals do not invade the space of higher-ranking members of the pack. We use the word *off* for no jumping because the word *down* applies to the lying-down position. To correct a dog for jumping, use a lead to deliver a consequence for the behavior.

A quick pop downward with the lead, until the dog's feet are on the ground, should provide enough correction to change his behavior.

Giving affection when the dog displays good manners, rather than when the dog acts out, reinforces your expectations for calm, self-restrained behavior.

To be in control of training situations, it can be beneficial to set up scenarios rather than waiting for them to happen naturally. To teach the "leave it" warning, this handler brought a distraction (pieces of hot dog) to the training location, so he could present the distraction and be prepared to respond without delay.

Get off Furniture

The concept of "off" can apply not only to jumping up on people but also to jumping on objects, such as the sofa or bed. From the dog's perspective, "off" should suggest getting back on the ground with four paws on the floor. This command applies whether your dog is permitted on furniture or whether she is forbidden that luxury.

If you plan to allow your dog on furniture, you should have a command that informs her she is to get back down on the floor immediately when you so instruct. In this training scenario, you may invite your dog onto the couch and allow her to get nice and comfy. Then do the following:

1. Use a lead connected to a collar that is able to provide a meaningful correction if she resists. Use her name, then the command "off."

2. If she doesn't immediately comply, use your lead and collar to provide a correction for noncompliance. The correction should be in the direction you want her to move, which is down toward the floor.

3. If the correction was above the threshold needed to change her behavior, when you repeat the exercise, she will get off the couch without the need for physical intervention.

4. If when repeating the scenario, your dog does not exit the sofa, increase the collar correction and pair it with a stronger presence and sense of expectation.

For dogs that are not allowed on furniture and therefore should not be invited upon it to teach the lesson, create a setting that better emulates your circumstances. Entice your dog to move toward the couch by placing a tasty treat or her favorite toy on the cushion. Or have someone whose lap your dog likes to invade sit on the sofa. Then do the following:

1. Use a lead and training collar capable of delivering a correction above the threshold to change behavior. As the dog begins to jump onto the couch, give the warning word "off" in a firm tone.

2. If the dog does not heed the warning, deliver an effective correction in the downward direction, which is opposite the infraction.

3. Repeat the scenario to determine whether your dog's behavior has changed based on the lesson.
4. If the dog chooses to jump up again, adjust the level of the correction and your attitude of authority to project your expectations.

Leave It

By now you may recognize that the Social Compliance Method is easy to apply to any behavior that you, as your dog's leader, find unacceptable. The "leave it" warning may be employed whether your dog is attempting to steal a used tissue from the waste basket, grab food under a child's highchair, or race after a squirrel.

This method requires that you pay attention and can recognize behaviors that your dog exhibits just prior to the unwanted action. Eyeing or moving toward food on the floor would be such an act. Correcting a dog that is in the act of eating food, chasing a cat, or stealing tissue is significantly more challenging than shutting down the dog while he is in the state of intention.

To establish your expectations for the "leave it" warning, follow the steps found in the two examples above, but use food on the floor or exposure to a cat or squirrel as the setup. It is critical that you do not allow the lead to become tight before you utter the warning words and deliver the correction.

The Most Important Skill for Dog Trainers

Developing the ability to proactively communicate your expectations to your dog may be the single, most important skill a good dog handler can develop. This talent is wholly dependent upon how well you pay attention to your dog's behavior.

THE BASICS

This chapter includes the four basic skills that all dogs should learn: sit, down, loose-lead walking, and come when called. They provide the foundation for more sophisticated tasks, such as retrieving. Teaching your dog to perform fun tricks or useful tasks is much easier when your dog understands and willingly performs the basic commands. The formal version of these same skills, which includes specific requirements for competitions, will be presented in the next chapter.

The Basic Sit

The remainder of this book is dedicated to providing detailed instruction and the philosophy behind a number of commands, useful skills, and fun tricks. The primary method used to teach the skill will be presented along with any alternate techniques that some people may find useful. Finally, when appropriate, the Comprehensive Method will explain how to impose very high standards for the behavior by correcting the dog when he doesn't comply. A correction method is not necessary to teach most of the skills. For folks who are seeking a high level of compliance, the Comprehensive Method explains how to transfer the behavior in the dog's mind to the "important social compliance" area of his brain.

Tip:

If you use a treat to teach your dog to perform exercises like sit, be prepared to eliminate the need for the food as soon as possible. The most complained about aspect of the Incentive Method is the fact the dog becomes reliant on the food to perform the task. That pitfall can be avoided by following a regimen of reducing the food rewards. If you aspire to very high level compliance, consider following up the Incentive Method with the Comprehensive Method to set a high standard of performance.

<u>Sit in Front</u>

To teach your dog to sit using the Incentive Method, hold a treat in front of and above his head. Say the dog's name, then command him to sit.

Move the treat upward and over the dog's head to lure his body into the sit position.

Deliver the treat once the dog places his rump on the ground. Then, offer praise.

Sit and Stay

The most basic command is "sit." Many people successfully teach their dogs to assume a sitting position quite easily using a luring method with a treat. Nearly as many people complain that although their dog will sit, he will not stay.

The traditional separation of the two commands (sit and stay) may be the reason that so many people fail to achieve their desired goal. In reality, there are few instances when "sit" should not also imply "stay sitting." When I teach a dog to sit, I do not typically use the word stay. The dog learns that when instructed to sit, she should stay there until directed to do something else.

However, if you enter an obedience competition, you will find that the two commands are considered distinct. The judge will instruct you to sit your dog and then leave your dog. When you leave your dog (whether in a group sit exercise or to move away during the recall exercise), you will be permitted to tell her to "stay." Curiously, if upon the "sit your dog" command, your dog were to sit and spring right back up again, the judge would not be able to continue the exercise until you were able to get your dog sitting again. Even though, in competitions, there is a distinction made between the sit and the stay command, there is an implication that once the dog is instructed to sit she will remain there.

In basic training, in order to make things simple, let's make the assumption that when you tell your dog to sit, lie down, or stand, it implies "stay" in that position. Therefore, you will be required to impart that information to your dog. Let's also assume that your dog does not know to stay unless you teach him that expectation. That will be the fairest way to go about training your dog.

Since "sit" is such a critical command, I will explain it in the greatest of detail.

With additional commands or tricks, less information will be required as each exercise builds on the skills that both you and your dog will develop during early training.

You may want your dog to sit in front of you, or you may want your dog to sit in the heel position. The heel position will be discussed in Chapter 6.

If you are using a bridge word or a clicker, from this point forward, when instructed to reward your dog, insert your bridge first, then give the reward.

Sit in Front

1. Position your dog in front of you in a standing position. You may need to take a step backward to help him get up if he is already sitting.
2. Hold a treat in your right hand.
3. In a kind but firm tone of voice, say your dog's name and the command "sit."
4. Allow your dog to see the treat in your right hand. Move your right hand in a sweeping motion from below the dog's chin to above his head, maintaining it centered between his eyes. Do not move it so high that he attempts to sit up or get up on his hind legs. Move it at a rate that will allow him to track its movement and move it high enough that he tilts his head backward. Then stop.
5. When your dog assumes the sitting position, deliver the reward.
6. At this early stage, we are shaping the behavior of moving from a stand to a sit. If your dog springs right back up again, it is acceptable.
7. If your dog does not sit, try again and focus on the speed and distance from the dog's face.

Struggling with the Food Reward?

If the dog is too excited about the food, consider using something that is less interesting, such as a piece of dry kibble.

If the dog is not interested enough, consider using a treat that will excite the dog, such as cheese, chicken, or liver treats.

The Alternate Sit Technique

If the dog needs additional help understanding your expectation, you may use a secondary technique along with the luring method or instead of it. You may gently tap or tuck the dog's rear end. Additionally, you may tug up on the dog's collar.

1. Position yourself so that the dog is on your left side rather than in front of you.
2. Hold the lead in your right hand and close to the collar.
3. Say the dog's name and the command word "sit."

Sometimes called the compulsion method, tugging up on your dog's collar while tapping his rear end toward the ground is an alternative to the incentive method.

Once your dog is sitting, praise him.

4. Gently tuck the dog's rump close to the base of his tail. Do not push on his spine.
5. Along with the rump tuck, you may also tug up on the dog's collar. Make certain that it is positioned very high on his neck.
6. Once he assumes the sit position, praise him verbally. You may deliver a treat, as long as you do so while he is still sitting.

Practice

1. Repeat the exercise several times over a few days until your dog is routinely sitting.
2. Begin removing the reward (treat or toy) over time.
3. Continue to provide verbal praise each time your dog sits.
4. Initially, remove about every tenth treat, then every fifth treat, then every other treat.
5. Mix up the frequency of treat delivery rather than actually counting since some dogs can learn to count, too!

Setting the Standard—"Sit" Means Stay

Once your dog demonstrates an understanding of the "sit" command, which should not take more than a few days, it's time to explain that "sit" means "stay there until I release you."

1. Adjust your dog's collar so that it is very high on his neck.
2. Put your lead in your left hand and hold it so there is very little slack. Avoid putting tension on your dog's neck.
3. Sit your dog by saying the dog's name and the word "sit."
4. Do not give the dog a treat at this time.
5. Watch your dog intently, but do not become tense in body or mind. Do not allow him to get up out of the sitting position.
6. Stay close to your dog.

7. If you perceive that he is about to break his sit position, tug upward on the lead. Do not get angry, frustrated, or irritated. You are simply teaching your dog about expectations that he is not yet aware of by offering feedback about his choice to get up.
8. Be proactive. Do not wait until your dog is standing before responding.
9. Do not speak. Do not repeat the "sit" command. Do not use his name. This is very important.

When you tell your dog to sit, it should be understood that he is to stay in place. To establish that standard, it is important to pay attention and proactively provide feedback to the dog about his behavior. In this photo, the handler is holding his left hand directly above the dog's collar so that, if necessary, he can give a collar correction. Notice that the lead is not tight on the dog's neck.

10. Along with an upwards tug on the collar, you may also gently touch his rump in the same way that may have been required when he first learned to sit.

11. Expect your dog to stay sitting for fifteen to thirty seconds, then calmly end the exercise. You may deliver a treat at this time, as long as he is still sitting. Immediately begin a regimen of intermittent rewards at this stage of the training. Do not give him a treat every time.

12. Give your release word in a relaxed manner. Do not excite him with an over-the-top song of praise. That teaches him to get up out of the sit just because you are happy with his behavior.

13. Repeat the exercise and add additional time before ending it.

Why You Shouldn't Chatter to Your Dog When Teaching the Sit Command

- If we want our dogs to learn to sit on the first command, we should not provide second, third, or fourth commands. That will teach him that he does not have to comply with the first command. Say it once, then make it happen.

- When your dog is learning, he is concentrating. Just as it's difficult for you to learn if someone is chatting at you, your dog needs time to process the information you are presenting. Providing clear, concise information without added frills gives your dog the best chance to learn the lesson.

Adding Distractions

Now that your dog is sitting on command and understands that he must stay or receive an upward collar tug, begin adding distractions. Since dogs are not a highly verbal species and instead use facial gestures and body posturing to communicate, your dog would prefer to "listen" to your body language rather than your spoken words. To help him learn spoken words better, you will want to make your body movements irrelevant to him. You should eventually be able to tell your dog to sit and have confidence that he will stay there while you perhaps open the door to take a package from a delivery person. You should be able to bend over to tie your shoe, clap your hands, or even do a little jig and your dog should remain sitting. If you want to compete in an obedience trial, your dog will have to stay sitting while you move 30 feet away for a minute or more. He must stay put even if another dog gets up and walks about in the trial arena.

Exercises to add distractions:

1. Sit your dog (say his name and use the command word "sit").

2. Hold the lead with just enough slack that your dog does not feel tension on his neck, but short enough to be able to immediately respond to any potential movement to get up out of the sit position.

3. Take a small step to the left and expect your dog to stay. Correct with a collar check if he does not.

4. Take a couple small steps to the right. Correct with a collar check if you perceive that your dog is about to get up.

5. Move back and forth in front of your dog. Remain calm and relaxed yet vigilant.

6. Hold the lead slightly above your dog's head so that at the slightest indication that he is considering getting up, you can provide feedback that he is to stay.

7. Move in a larger and larger arch around your dog until you can actually walk a full circle around him. You may need to gently touch his head or shoulders the first time you walk completely around him. This is just to let him know you are in contact with him, not to correct him. Use the leash to give an upward tug if you think he is going to get up.

8. Bend over and touch your knees or your toes. Do a jumping jack. Wave your arms over your head. Stomp your feet. Whistle. Sing. Jump around. All the while you are doing these actions, be prepared to give a collar check if your dog begins to get up.

By this time, if you have been paying attention to your dog, you will have become quite good at observing and acting proactively. Dogs have a great deal of respect for people who present themselves as highly proactive because it is a necessary skill of a good leader. You will find that the required intensity of the collar tug correction will not be as strong as it may have been when you first introduced the concept to your dog. This is a good thing. If you find that your dog continues to break the sit position, you are probably not providing information above the threshold to change his behavior. You are essentially nagging your dog rather than actually correcting him. If this is the case, you may need to adjust the collar higher on your dog's neck, use more force when actually correcting him, or deliver a more potent collar check correction. It should not take more than three or four 10- to 15-minute training sessions before your dog is demonstrating a very high level of understanding that "sit" means sit, no matter what. If you project frustration, anger, disappointment, or frantic energy when attempting to correct your dog, the physical action will have significantly less effect than if you remain calm and composed.

Becoming Free

The next stage in teaching a reliable sit is to drop the lead. Do this in a very nonchalant manner. If you were paying good attention and preventing your dog from getting up out of the sit all the while you added distractions, the act of dropping the lead should not come as a surprise to your dog. If you avoided using the leash as a restraining device, letting go of it should be fairly insignificant to both you and the dog. At this stage, you may begin walking farther from the dog. Remember to avoid giving any additional commands. Once you tell him to sit, your dog should expect that you will back up your demands without providing a second or third command.

Increase your expectations by walking farther from the dog, turning your back on him, sitting in a chair across the room, or briefly stepping out of sight. In the beginning, do this for very short periods of time before moving back to a point where you could pick up the lead or gently touch him on the head. The goal is to move without allowing him to get up out of the sit position. Remain as close as necessary to help your dog understand that he is still under your influence of authority.

The Basic Down

Down can be a challenging position for some dogs to achieve, especially those that have not fully surrendered to the influence of their humans. While the Incentive Method can be used to teach dogs to move into the actual position, for most dogs, the Comprehensive Method will set the standard for behavior.

Using the Incentive Method for Down

1. Position your dog in a sit, either directly in front of you or on your left side.
2. Hold a treat in your right hand.

Dogs read us. It is what they do for a living. They can sense when we trust them. As you move farther from your dog during training, it is critical that you give the impression of trust in his behavior. When dropping the lead, do not make a big production out of the event. If you are concerned about whether or not your dog will stay sitting, you can step on the end of the lead. Stepping away from your dog for the first time can give you a big boost of confidence in the training work you have done. However, when you return to your dog, do not make a big fuss about what you have just accomplished. You don't want your dog to think it is out of the ordinary for you to walk some distance from him, so don't make a big deal about returning to him. *Lynn Watson/Shutterstock*

3. In a kind but firm tone of voice, say your dog's name and the word "down."
4. Allow your dog to see the treat in your right hand. Move your right hand in a sweeping motion from around the dog's nose level to the ground between her front legs. Move it at a rate that will allow her to track its movement and follow it to the floor.
5. When your dog assumes the down position, deliver the reward.
6. At this early stage, we are shaping the behavior of moving from a sit to a down. If your dog springs right back up again, it is acceptable.
7. If your dog does not lie down, try again. Focus on your speed and distance from the dog's nose. Make certain to hold the treat stationary on the ground, 6 to 12 inches from your dog's front feet.

The Alternate Technique for Down

If your dog needs additional help understanding your expectation, you may use a secondary technique, either along with the luring method or in exchange of it. You may physically guide the dog into the down position.

1. Position your dog on your left side.
2. Hold the lead in your right hand, close to the collar, or insert your right thumb or fingers into the dog's collar, under her chin.
3. Look down at your dog and assess whether she has rocked onto a hip. If she has, it will be very easy to guide her into the down position. If she has not rocked onto a hip, consider gently touching her between the shoulder and the loin area (just in front of her rear legs by her stomach) to help rock her onto a hip.

4. Place your left hand on the dog's shoulder opposite the hip onto which she has rocked.
5. Say the dog's name and the command word "down."
6. While gently pushing or tapping on the shoulder with your left hand, tug downward on the collar to guide the dog into the down position.
7. Once she is down, praise her verbally. You may deliver a food reward as long as she is still in the down position.
8. During the shaping of this behavior, we will not expect the dog to stay in the down position.

Practice
1. Repeat the exercise several times over a few days until your dog is routinely lying down on command.
2. Begin removing the reward (treat or toy) over time.
3. Initially, remove about every tenth treat. Then remove every fifth treat, then every other treat.
4. Mix up the frequency of treat delivery, since some dogs can learn to count!
5. Continue to provide verbal praise each time your dog lies down.

Setting the Standard—"Down" Means Stay

Once your dog demonstrates an understanding of the "down" command, which should not take more than a few days, it's time to explain that "down" means "stay there until I release you."

1. Sit your dog on your left side.
2. Command her to lie down.
3. Once she is in the down position, step on the lead close to her collar. This may be between the front legs of a larger dog or to the side of her legs for a small dog.
4. Stand up, keeping your foot on the lead and your eyes on your dog.

Basic Down

To lure your dog into a down position, present a treat close to his nose.

Move the treat downward toward the dog's front feet.

Pull the treat outward, away from the dog's front feet.

Deliver the treat only when the dog's elbows are on the ground.

Basic Down

This dog is not rocked onto his hip but is sitting squarely on his haunches. Teaching the down with physical assistance should emulate the natural way your dog lies down. Many dogs rock onto a hip prior to lying down. Helping them into the position makes using a physical method of training much easier for both the dog and the handler.

Here, Perry has been rocked onto his hip in preparation for the final "down" command. To help your dog rock onto a hip, gently apply pressure around the dog's loin area with your left hand.

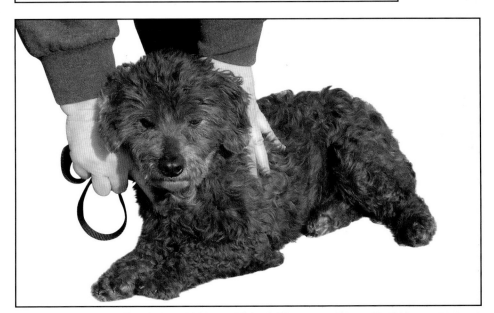

Once your dog is comfortably rocked onto his hip, your left hand shifts up toward his shoulder. While your right hand tugs down on the collar under the dog's chin, your left hand rocks the dog over at the shoulder. When you perform this exercise properly, the dog simply melts into a down position. He shows no signs of distress and does not protest.

"Down" Means Stay

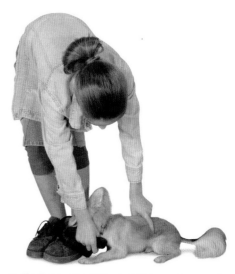

Unlike the Incentive Method, which lures a dog toward a treat, an alternate method uses physical touch to help a dog assume the down position. This method lets the handler back up his or her expectations if the dog attempts to rise before the release command. Using physical intervention to communicate standards in this way does not surprise a dog, since it emulates the method used to teach the exercise.

When the dog lies down, stepping on the lead close to the collar can provide added insurance that she will remain down. However, it is still the job of the handler to watch the dog's intentions and respond with feedback if the dog begins to get up.

5. If you perceive that she is about to break her down position, your first line of defense is already in place. If she rises up on her elbows, she will receive a collar correction because you are stepping on the leash. However, you may also need to reach down and touch her on the shoulders, or reach for the lead and give a quick collar correction under her chin.

6. Be proactive. Do not wait until your dog is standing before responding.

7. Do not speak. Do not repeat the "sit" command. Do not use her name. This is very important.

When the dog begins to get up, use the same type of touch to correct his behavior as you did when teaching the down.

Millie is an eight-month-old German shepherd dog that had a cat chasing habit. Once she understood the meaning of the command word "down," and she realized her handler's expectations to remain down once instructed to do so, the Comprehensive Method was used to teach her that cat chasing was no longer acceptable.

8. Expect your dog to stay in the down position for thirty seconds to a few minutes (depending upon the dog), then end the exercise.

9. You may deliver a treat at this time, as long as she is still lying down.

10. Begin a regimen of intermittent rewards at this stage of the training. Do not give a treat every time.

11. Give your release word in a calm, relaxed manner.

12. Repeat the exercise, adding additional time in the down position before ending the exercise.

Adding Distractions

Once your dog demonstrates that she understands your expectation for the down exercise, you should begin to add distractions. Do this in the same manner as with the sit command. When it is no longer necessary for you to step on the lead, you may begin to step to the left and right and circle your dog. Develop your skill to become very observant of the precursor behaviors that your dog presents just before she tries to get up. This may be a tipping down of her head or a rolling of her shoulders. Provide a meaningful correction as a consequence if she starts to stand up.

Ask a friend to create distractions, such as running a vacuum cleaner around your dog while you reinforce your expectations that she remains down. Have someone ring the doorbell, toss treats on the floor around your dog, or ride by on a skateboard. Remain calm and vigilant. Try your best to influence your dog proactively while she is in the state of intention of getting up, rather than after she is up and lunging at the skateboard or the cat. When you use a correction method, you will not have to apply as strong a collar tug when your dog is still thinking about breaking her command rather than once she is already chasing the cat.

Basic Loose-Lead Walking

I respect that every dog is different and that each owner may choose to impose different standards for his or her dog's behavior. At the same time, I very strongly recommend that all dog owners employ two zero tolerance policies:

1. No canine teeth on human flesh.
2. No pulling.

While it is fairly easy for most folks to understand the no-biting rule, many people do not realize the extreme importance of establishing and enforcing a no-pulling principle. Simply put, the dog that is out in front considers himself the leader. Therefore, when we allow our dog to pull ahead of us, we are granting him the position of the top dog. If we expect our dog to be respectful and social, it sends a very ambiguous signal every time we behave in a way that conflicts with those objectives.

The dog that is allowed to take a position in front of his owner typically will assume the responsibilities of the pack leader. After all, the handler assumes the follower rank simply by the position he or she adopts. Canine leadership behaviors include establishing the path of travel and panning for threats. When you allow your dog to put his nose to the ground and pull you along, you are supporting the notion that he has the authority to determine where you will trek and how quickly you will travel.

Additionally, the dog that is allowed to pull ahead of his owner will often feel compelled to scan for monsters and other perceived perils. He will be on high alert, and every blowing leaf, squirrel, bicyclist, or jogger could be considered to be worthy of battle. After all, as a dog, your companion cannot truly triumph over such hazards so he may adopt the bite-first-ask-questions-later

When walking from point A to point B, the handler and dog should be calm and composed. The dog should not pull ahead or pan for threats. Notice the handler's relaxed left arm and the tranquil expression on the dog's face. Walking a dog that has been trained to walk properly on a lead will feel like walking a feather.

Jane is training her border collie, Ace, to compete at herding trials. There are few other venues where it is as important that the dog projects a sense of self-restraint. Sheep and other livestock quickly assess whether a dog seems composed and collected. If they suspect the dog is not in control of himself, sheep will become unnerved, often to the point of acting out during the trial.

If your dog has never been on a leash before or has developed a habit of serious pulling against the leash, review the information in Chapter 4 on breaking a dog to a lead. Once your dog can remain calm under the umbrella of your authority and stand calmly next to you while on a lead, it is time to add the act of migrating, or loose-lead walking.

philosophy in order to keep you, his worthy follower, safe from harm.

Hopefully, that is not the calm state of mind in which you would like your dog to exist. The best way to combat the problem is to implement a follower status for your dog. Followers do not lead. Therefore, you must not allow your dog to assume a position in front of your body when you walk. Followers also do not disrespect their leader by pulling against their authority. We must first establish the position in which we will tolerate our follower dog to occupy, then we must address any desire on his part to pull ahead.

Because walking properly while on a leash is truly a state of mind, rather than a command we might teach our dog (like sit or down), the only method we will employ is the Social Compliance Method. The dog will receive a correction for exceeding a barrier that we set.

Competitive heeling, which will be presented in Chapter 6, requires a dog to have a keen sense of position relative to his handler. Loose-lead walking has slightly less stringent requirements. For example, the dog can walk on the left or right side of the handler. However, in keeping with the expectation that the dog will not assume the leadership role, he must remain behind the plane of the handler's knees and may not sniff out the path of travel. The dog should be expected to consider the entire process of walking on a lead as

a task that he must perform within a set of guidelines his handler will set for him.

When the dog is asked to walk on the handler's left side, the customary command word is "heel." When teaching a dog to walk on the right side, a second command word, such as "right" or "side," can be used. Teaching your dog how to walk properly is a bit like playing the child's board game Operation. As long as you hold the metal forceps within the allotted space, you have smooth sailing. But if you touch the sides, the red light flashes and the buzzer sounds, alerting you that you have exceeded the acceptable limits.

When walking on a lead, as long as the dog is in the correct position, the walk should be a pleasant experience. But if he pulls ahead, reaches down to grab a chicken bone in the alley, lunges at a passing dog, or chooses to balk, he will receive a negative consequence. If that correction is above the threshold to stimulate the dog's desire to avoid the negative experience, the dog will quickly learn the expectations for walking properly on a loose lead.

Steps to creating a dog that walks well on a lead:

1. Before walking, let your dog know your plan by saying his name and giving the command "heel."
2. Use a well-fitted collar to deliver a quick correction when the dog starts to pull ahead of your knees; attempts to sniff the ground; lunges or pulls to the side; focuses on an object of desire, such as a cat, squirrel, or skateboarder (you may add the "leave it" warning at this time); or attempts to grab food or other objects along the path.
3. When you come to a street crossing or other stop, tell your dog to sit or lie down using the techniques described in Chapters 6 and 7. Remember: If you say it, make it happen.

4. Before walking again, use the "heel" command so that your dog knows he is no longer required to sit or lie down.

Sometimes a walk is also used as the time the dog is expected to relieve himself. In this scenario, it is recommended that the dog walks properly with the handler to a designed location. There, the handler can give the dog the freedom to walk about and sniff for the best potty spot. While the dog will be allowed to sniff, he should not be allowed to pull on the lead. This is one instance where a retractable lead can come in handy. Once the dog has done his duty, continued walking on lead should be accomplished as a task, with the dog being corrected for unacceptable behaviors, such as alerting the presence of a squirrel, barking at another dog, sniffing, grabbing for trash on the path, or otherwise disrespecting the process of walking properly as a good follower.

Come When Called

Many people struggle when teaching their dog to reliably come back to them. While the Incentive Method can be used to explain the meaning behind the word "come," the Comprehensive Method is essential to enlighten the dog about the standards of performance that will be expected.

The Incentive Method is most valuable when employed with puppies under four months old. Young puppies are in a life stage where they find value in seeking the security of an authority figure. Add a morsel of food to the equation, and the puppy will quickly learn to come running to the command word. However, once the puppy moves into adolescence, the desire to explore and need to develop some self-reliance can turn the perfect puppy into a teenage terror.

When it comes to young puppies, the best way to teach the meaning behind the command word is simple.

1. While sitting on the floor near the puppy (no farther than 3 feet), hold out a delectable treat close to the puppy's nose.
2. When the puppy focuses on the treat, say her name and the word "come" in a happy tone of voice.
3. Bring your arm toward your lap, luring the puppy toward you.
4. When the puppy gets close enough to touch, praise her profusely and deliver the treat.
5. Repeat the exercise many times, slowly increasing the distance the puppy must travel to get to you before receiving the treat.
6. If you have a partner, work together to call the puppy back and forth between you, slowly increasing the distance the puppy must travel.
7. Once the puppy will come across a room, move to an outdoor setting. Start over at the same distance that was successful in step 1.
8. Repeat all steps outdoors.

Once your puppy is around sixteen weeks old, you should expect that she may no longer come when called to a food incentive. The world is full of more pleasurable delights than your treat or your praise, and at four to six months old, your puppy learns about all those diversions. In this regard, your job is to keep her alive through exceptional management during that time, rather than expect absolute compliance. It is contrary to her level of maturity to do otherwise.

Once a pup turns six months old, she will be moving into the life stage where she can handle essential consequences for unacceptable behavior. At that time, the Comprehensive Method can be used to create a reliable recall.

There are three rules that must be followed to ensure a successful recall command:

Rule 1

Just as you must make your dog sit for her to understand the "sit" command and to set your standards, you must make your dog come when given this command. The reason people often fail when teaching the recall is that they do not have control over the dog when they say the command word. The dog learns to ignore the word as it has no meaning.

In the beginning, your dog must be on lead to learn the meaning of "come." You should say, "Fluffy, come!" then give the lead a tug if the dog does not immediately begin coming towards you. Once the dog is moving towards the handler, if he decides to move in any other direction due to a distraction, the handler should give another tug attempting to correct the dog for noncompliance with enough intensity to get above the threshold to change the dog's behavior and not nag the dog. The lead should never be tight. The dog must not be reeled in like a fish but be allowed to feel the comfort of a loose lead unless he is getting a collar check for disobedience.

Before your dog understands the meaning of "come," if he is not on a lead, use a different command, such as "here," "that'll do," or "let's go," any time you are not able to absolutely reinforce the command. That way, if your dog chooses not to come, he is not disobeying the actual recall command. This system applies only during the initial training phase.

Rule 2

Regardless of whether a dog runs across two interstate highways, kills a skunk, eats your neighbor's prize tomatoes, or swims in a stinky pond, once she arrives to you, you must always love her and praise her for coming. For some people, this is one of the most difficult rules to follow. But just as you would not want to go to your boss's office if he scolded you every time you entered, your dog will have no interest in coming to you if she knows she's going to get punished. Punishment can take the form of words, actions, or negative feelings that you project. If you are disappointed in your dog, she can feel that sentiment. Dogs, like humans, move toward pleasant experiences and feelings and move away from negative or unpleasant feelings. If you want to create a dog that comes willingly and readily, you must make the experience positive and pleasant, even in less-than-perfect circumstances.

Rule 3

A dog that is poorly managed or is not social (as in one that has no respect for his human's authority) is not easy to train. If your dog has little or no reverence for her human's position as pack leader, she will have little need to obey any command, including "come." Establishing and practicing leadership on a daily basis is very important.

Here are the steps for teaching a reliable recall:

1. Use a training collar that fits high on your dog's neck.

No Nagging!

When using a correction method, it is critical to remember that nagging your dog will result in an unhappy partner that will spend energy on resisting your authority. Avoid nagging by correcting above the threshold required to change your dog's behavior. Confirm that your dog's collar is fitted high on his neck and always remain calm and controlled when correcting your dog.

2. Use a long line to ensure that you will be able to make your dog come when you say the command word.

3. Have a helper entertain your dog by petting, playing with a toy, or even delivering some tasty food in small amounts.

4. Hold the end of the long line and move 6 to 10 feet from the dog (increase distance with time).

5. In a pleasant voice, say your dog's name, followed by the command "come."

6. If the dog does not come, give a meaningful correction for lack of compliance by tugging the lead.

7. Once the dog is coming toward you, you may give verbal encouragement.

8. When your dog gets to you, lavish her with praise.

9. Repeat in many different scenarios, especially those in which your dog once refused to come to you.

The lead is never to be used as a restraint device. Its function is simply to deliver a correction if the dog fails to comply with your command to come. If you are concerned that your dog will only come when on lead, follow these instructions. They are designed to make the lead insignificant to the exercise by shifting the dog's attention away from the position where the lead was first placed.

1. Follow steps 1 through 4 above.

2. Drop the lead on the ground. Leave the lead where it lies and walk 10 to 20 feet away.

This twelve-week-old border collie puppy has learned to come running for a treat.

Three Rules for Come When Called

1. When you say "come," you must make it happen.
2. Once your dog gets to you, you must love on the dog and praise her profusely.
3. Practice leadership on a daily basis. A dog that disrespects her owner will not learn to come when off lead.

3. Bend over as if you are picking up another lead from the ground.
4. Walk 10 to 20 feet in another direction. Bend over as if you are picking up yet another lead from the ground.
5. Move all around in a random pattern until you end up back where you left the real lead on the ground. Pick up the lead.
6. Complete steps 5 through 9 above.

If you have been working on a reliable sit or down with your dog, you may exchange the role with the assistance of a partner to keep your dog occupied with the command to sit or down.

As with all exercises, you may slowly eliminate the need for a lead by cutting the long line down in size or by using a shorter leash. This will provide a bit of extra insurance once your dog demonstrates a high level of compliance with the command. You may remove the lead when your dog is working at a high level of reliability in a variety of situations with many distractions. The more you practice, the better your dog will become. Do not shy away from situations where distractions vie for your dog's attention. Those are exactly the locations where you should practice.

When teaching the recall, refrain from using any body signals, such as bending at the waist, slapping your thighs, or clapping to encourage your dog to come. You may need to call your dog when she cannot see you. Teach her to pay attention to just your voice by eliminating any physical cues she may choose to use instead. Otherwise, she will rely on your body cues rather than spoken words. This is especially important if you plan to compete in obedience trials. There, you will not be able to give any additional physical signals along with your verbal command.

Practice the recall command often and in different locations, especially in locations where your dog previously failed to come. Follow the mantra "Say it, then make it happen." Always praise your dog when she comes. Never get angry with her or punish her once she arrives. Present her with increasingly difficult distractions, always demanding compliance to the recall command. Practice sound leadership on a daily basis.

COMPETITION SKILLS

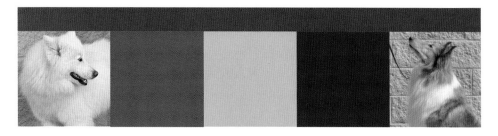

Heeling is the exercise that separates the cream from the milk.

Once you have mastered the basic skills, you may want to enter your dog into competitions. It's a great way to display all the work you have accomplished while training your dog. This chapter contains instructions on how to teach your dog to perform the exercises required in the Novice level. Scoring at an obedience trial focuses on the teamwork between the dog and the handler. You will also find information about how to best handle your dog during competition, as well as the judge's expectations in each exercise.

Competition Heeling

I believe that the most important exercise in competition obedience is heeling. By and large, the other exercises are scored in a close to all-or-nothing format. Heeling is the exercise that separates the cream from the milk. If your dog shows great heeling ability, you stand a great chance of doing well in the competition. While other exercises offer opportunities for point loss for minor infractions, such as a crooked sit after the recall exercise or moving a foot during the stand, none compares to the range of possible point deductions involved in heeling.

Proper heel position is rooted in tradition. The first organized competitions involved hunters and their sporting dogs. Most hunters hold a gun in the right hand. To keep dogs safe when shooting a duck or quail, hunters traditionally kept their dogs on the left. Thus, hunting trial rules defined the heel position. Later, people created competitive obedience trials. They used the heel position as the starting and ending points of exercises.

In AKC competitions (and therefore in 4-H competitions, since 4-H has adopted AKC rules), during heeling, a handler may hold her left arm across her waist, as in this photo, or allow it to swing freely at her side. Using the left hand to lure the dog to stay in heel position is not permitted.

During a competition, proper heel position is required whether the dog is standing, sitting, lying down, or moving next to the handler. The dog should be on the handler's left side, straight in line with the direction the handler is facing. The area from the dog's head to its shoulder should be in line with the handler's hip. The dog shouldn't be crowding the handler, nor too far away, and should allow for the handler to have freedom of motion at all times.

If you have a competitive nature and want to excel in obedience competitions, it is imperative that your dog excels at heeling.

Prior to competition heeling, your dog should be tolerant of working on a lead (see Chapter 4) and have experience walking on a loose lead (see Chapter 5). Competition heeling is somewhat like a dance that the handler and the dog perform. As the handler, you are the leader of the dance. The dog should take subtle cues from you about your path of travel and should adjust accordingly in an attempt to remain in the heel position while you move around the ring under the judge's commands. In rally obedience competitions, there is no judge calling the shots. Your course of travel is defined by signs along the course.

Rally obedience competitions might require dozens of other skills, including a moving side step, a halt and down, and serpentine travel around a series of cones. But it should be noted that a dog that is exceptional at heeling will be best prepared for and highly rewarded in rally classes.

The Social Compliance Method, which uses corrections for behaviors that are not socially acceptable, can be used to teach a dog that pulling on the lead, sniffing the ground while walking, or lunging at a passing squirrel is unacceptable. The Social Compliance Method taps into a dog's basic understanding that respect for leadership is expected. The root behaviors that support competitive heeling are grounded in the Social Compliance techniques.

However, the Social Compliance Method is not acceptable for teaching exercises that do not make sense to the dog's natural desire

The standard commands from judge to competitor in competition obedience are:

- Forward: Walk forward in a straight line
- Halt: Come to a stop in a natural manner within a few steps
- Left turn: Turn 90 degrees to the left
- Right turn: Turn 90 degrees to the right
- Fast: The handler should run and the dog should adjust pace accordingly to remain in heel position
- Slow: The handler must decrease speed to a noticeably slower pace
- Normal pace: The handler returns to the original pace after performing a Fast or a Slow
- About turn: The handler does a right about turn resulting in travel 180 degrees from the previous direction

to be accepted into a pack. I consider "perfect heel position" to be challenging for a dog to understand, since, in nature, a dog need only respect his leader's position and status, and stay in follower mode. But he does not have to remain in a perfect formation. With exercises that make little sense to the dog, the Incentive Method can help fill the gap in understanding.

To help your dog comprehend such exact requirements as the perfect heel position, rewarding him when he is there can be a significant learning experience. The reward should not be used to bribe the dog into heeling for food but instead should compensate him when he achieves the desired position. If the dog presents any unacceptable behaviors, such as dropping his nose to the ground to sniff or alerting to a distraction like a passing cat, the correction-based method can be applied. The more proactive you are at catching your dog in the stage of intention, where he is about to sniff rather than is already sniffing, the less intense the correction needs to be. After receiving a correction for distraction, if the dog moves back to the perfect heel position,

he can receive a reward. This combination of using corrections for disobedience and rewards for achieving high compliance defines the Comprehensive Method.

In some competitions, you will be allowed to say only your dog's name and the word "heel" once before each halt. You will need to teach your dog to perform turns, speed changes, and sits when you stop without verbal or physical commands.

Teaching Heeling—Forward and Halt

Begin with your dog sitting in the heel position.

1. You may want to start each exercise with a crisp "ready!" (see sidebar.)
2. Say your dog's name, then the command word "heel."
3. Step off at a normal pace, walking as straight and steady as possible.
4. To project a confident attitude to your dog and the judge, make an effort to look ahead with your shoulders back, chin up, and straight posture.
5. When preparing to come to a halt, attempt to do so in a smooth and consistent manner.
6. As you come to a stop, say your dog's name and the command "sit." Help your dog sit, if necessary, using methods described in Chapter 5. While you will not be able to command the dog to sit in competition, it is helpful to do so in the beginning.
7. Repeat.

During competitive heeling, the judge will take off points for a handler who guides his or her dog with the leash. Lagging, forging ahead, and crowding the handler will also result in minor to substantial deductions. Crooked sits or failure to sit also lead to deductions.

Using the Rules to Your Benefit

In most competitions, prior to commanding you to heel your dog or perform other exercises, the judge must ask, "Are you ready?" Since you are expected to respond to the judge, you may take advantage of the situation to alert your dog that you are about to begin working. Rather than simply nodding your head or saying "yes" under your breath, reply to the judge with a clear, upbeat "ready!" Prior to attending the trials, you can teach your dog that "ready" means "Wake up, we are about to start working!"

Competition heeling begins with the dog sitting. Handlers should stand with good posture and focus ahead. In doing so, they show their dogs the direction they will travel and reinforce that the dogs are in follower mode.

Healing — Forward and Halt

When heeling, step off with confidence.

Walk at a brisk pace. Points can be deducted if the dog lags behind the handler or if the handler guides the dog.

When preparing to stop, tell the dog to "sit." This extra command is necessary during training but must be eliminated before competition.

During training, reward the dog for a quick, straight sit.

Use an appropriate level of correction any time your dog begins to stray from the heel position. Tug backward toward her tail if she begins to forge ahead. Tug upward if she attempts to sniff the ground. Combine the corrections with lavish praise when your dog is in proper heel position. You may use happy tones of voice or deliver small tidbits of food when your dog is in the exact position you desire.

Refrain from speaking, especially in sweet, coddling tones, when your dog is not in proper heel position. While it may seem natural to coach your dog from the wrong position (such as lagging behind you) into the proper position, it can lead to a confused and poorly performing dog. When a dog hears praise tones, she will pair that affection with the behavior she is presenting at that exact moment in time. If she is lagging behind and you say "Come on girl. That a gal. Get up here" with a sweet, praising quality, she may interpret that you find her actions acceptable, even that you are very pleased with her lagging position.

An alternate approach to simply taking off and walking at full speed, right off the bat, is to break the exercise down into very small increments:

1. Begin with your dog in heel position.
2. Say the dog's name and the word "heel."
3. Take just one step and halt.
4. Help the dog sit.
5. Say the dog's name and "heel."
6. Take just one step and halt.
7. Help the dog sit.
8. Repeat with just one step at a time for six to ten steps.
9. Say the dog's name, say "heel," and take two steps.
10. Help the dog sit.
11. Repeat five to ten times.
12. Add one or two extra steps before the halt and sit.

The value in this method is that it does not allow the dog to forge ahead, lag behind, sniff, or otherwise present behavior that is not heeling and warrants correction. It keeps the dog's attention.

Teaching Turns (Left, Right, About)

Once your dog is heeling nicely in straight lines, you should add left, right, and about turns. Consider heeling as dancing with your dog. The more consistent you are with your footwork and the method in which you move the rest of your body, the easier it will be for your dog to learn to stay in heel position when you change directions. Sometimes it can be helpful to practice turns without your dog until you can move your feet consistently each time you execute the same turn.

How you move your feet is less important than remaining consistent each time you turn. But remember that since your dog is on your left side, he is more apt to key in on your left foot, ankle, knee, hip, or shoulder than another part of your body to decide when you are about to turn. Try to execute your turns as squarely as possible without appearing mechanical or unnatural. Do not cut the corners.

Performing the about turn properly will allow your dog the space to turn with you and not be left behind. If, when you turn, you keep your knees directly above your ankles, your hips directly above your knees, and your shoulders directly above your hips, your body will form a column around which your dog can wrap his body. Consider the about turn an action that you must accomplish while standing on top of a 12-inch square tile, like you might find on a kitchen floor.

Teaching Changes in Pace

During competition heeling, the judge will tell you to "fast" or "slow." In order to earn the total available points, you must demonstrate that your dog will change pace with you. When performing the "fast," you should jog and your change of pace must be noticeable. When performing the "slow," you should slow your rate enough that your dog will need to change her gait. When the judge says, "normal pace," you are to return to your standard speed. Your dog should remain in heel position at the speed changes.

Turns

The about turn should be executed at the same pace you are walking during heeling. The rules do not permit judges to require an about turn at the fast or slow pace. Practice maintaining your tempo when performing the 180-degree about turn.

Whereas loose-lead walking has just a few rules, competition heeling is more like ballroom dancing. Your ability to remain consistent with your footwork, posture, pace, and attitude will all contribute to your dog's understanding of the stylized version of taking a walk.

Once you have fully executed the about turn and are facing 180 degrees from your last direction of travel, focus forward and step off with confidence. Many handlers teach their dogs to lag during the about turn because they slow down to wait for the dogs.

The Figure-Eight Exercise

The figure eight is a heeling exercise and is typically included in the heeling score rather than existing as a standalone exercise. It provides the opportunity to demonstrate that your dog is able to remain in heel position while you move around posts in a figure-eight pattern.

As you circle the post on your right side, your dog will need to increase his speed relative to yours in order to remain in heel position. As you circle the post on your left side, the dog must slow his relative pace, since the radius of his circle will be smaller than yours. The judge will also command you to halt a couple of times while you perform the figure eight. The basic principles of excellent heeling drive the training of this exercise. Some dogs require a lure of food in the beginning to learn that they must speed up and move faster than the handler to perform the outside circle. Other dogs may require a solid correction to

Figure Eight

The figure-eight exercise begins with the handler and dog stationed halfway between the two posts and about 1 or 2 feet behind the midline. The first step can be in a forward direction, followed by a diagonal course around the first post.

You may go either way around the posts. Maintaining a consistent speed is of paramount importance, even more so than straight heeling. This exercise tests your dog's ability to remain in heel position, even if she must speed up or slow down to do so.

There are no about turns or changes of pace in the figure eight. The judge's orders to the competitors are "forward" and "halt." The judge must order at least one halt in the middle of the exercise and one at the end.

Halts can occur anywhere along the figure-eight course. Teach your dog to stop in proper heel position, even if you are circling a post and she is speeding up or slowing down to maintain pace with you.

Watch Me

Starting in a sitting position allows you to be closer to your dog. Direct your dog's gaze into your eyes, then immediately reward the behavior.

To teach the "watch" command, use high-value treats to capture your dog's attention.

Repeat the lesson from a standing position.

Performing the "watch" command in the "front" position is useful during many obedience exercises.

As the final product of a methodical approach, a dog no longer requires incentives to look up to his handler during heeling.

prevent forging ahead when executing the inside circle.

The "posts" are human stewards who stand 8 feet apart. While you can practice the exercise using a couple of chairs or traffic cones, don't forget to include some training with real people. Some dogs will feel a need to sniff or otherwise be distracted by human posts. In my 4-H fair prep class, kids and their dogs act as posts. In this way, the dogs learn to remain calm and composed in heel position while other dogs and humans move past them. This is excellent practice for the sit-stay exercise.

Watch Me

A successful method to help your dog stay in heel position during competitions is to teach her to "watch." For some dogs it seems to go against nature to look at the handler while walking forward, so she must learn to trust you while walking with her head turned in towards your body or up towards your face. Take your time with teaching this skill and practice it in a variety of situations.

A dog that heels with her head turned in, looking intently at the handler, is presenting a stylized version of the exercise. But it is highly valued in some organizations. A judge should not penalize a dog that does not gaze into her handler's eyes while heeling. However, many competitors find it not only an appealing appearance, but it can also serve a utilitarian purpose. The dog that is focused on watching her handler is less likely to be distracted by disturbances in the obedience trial arena.

Teaching the Watch

1. Sit in a chair with your dog sitting in front of you.
2. Say your dog's name and "watch" (or whatever word you would like to designate this behavior).
3. Move a fairly high-value treat from your

chest level to your eyes (or wherever you want your dog to look during the watch command).
4. The instant your dog gazes into your eyes, give the reward (or use the bridge-and-reward method).
5. Repeat this exercise many times, rewarding your dog when she makes eye contact.
6. Move to a standing position with your dog directly in front of you and repeat the sequence above.
7. Place your dog in heel position and repeat the sequence. This time, the dog will have to turn her head toward your body and face to perform the watch.

Setting the Standard for Watch

To achieve a highly reliable "watch" command, once your dog is performing the exercise reliably at least 80 percent of the time and once you have begun to reduce the frequency of your rewards, you may use the Comprehensive Method.

1. Sit with your dog positioned in front of you.
2. Instruct your dog to watch.

Reminder Time

It's time to remind you that a correction should not be paired with any negative emotions. You should not be angry or frustrated with your dog when you correct her. You are simply providing meaningful information that her behavior is not acceptable. If your correction is delivered above the threshold required to change her behavior, she will demonstrate self-restraint regarding your expectations.

3. Have a helper present a distraction by making a noise or tossing a tennis ball.
4. If your dog turns toward the distraction, use a quick collar check to correct him.
5. When your dog turns back to watch you, reward him with verbal praise or a treat.
6. Repeat the exercise. If your dog ignores the distraction when it is presented, reward him with verbal praise or a treat. If he is still distracted, correct him, but avoid nagging.
7. Repeat the exercise in a number of different scenarios with increasingly challenging distractions.
8. Repeat the exercise when you are sitting with your dog in front, when you are standing with your dog in front, and when you are standing with your dog in heel position.

Stand for Exam

The purpose of the stand exercise is to demonstrate that your dog can be examined by a stranger (the judge) without showing resentment. In the lower classes of 4-H competition, this exercise is performed on a 6-foot lead. In the regular AKC novice class, the lead is removed before the exercise starts. The exercise begins with your dog sitting in heel position. When the judge says "Stand your dog and leave when you are ready," you may take the time you need and handle your dog as necessary to help him into a standing position. Once your dog is standing to your satisfaction, instruct him to stay. Walk to the end of your lead or 6 feet away and turn and face the dog. At that time, the judge will step up to your dog and touch it gently on the head, the shoulders, and the rump. Then the judge will move back. When the judge commands, return to your dog, walking around behind him to the right and into heel position.

During the exercise, your dog must remain standing and not move his feet from the original position they were in when you left him. He should not shy away or cower from the judge.

Teaching the stand requires quite a bit of patience, since it is the stance that dogs assume before they walk or run off. It is unlike the sit or down position, which dogs assume when they plan to stay somewhere for a while. Therefore, it is advisable to have already trained your dog to sit and lie down, so that he understands the concept of staying in place under your authority.

Step by Step—Moving from Sit to Stand

1. Begin with your dog sitting in the heel position.
2. Ready your left hand near the dog's loin area.
3. Present a fairly high-value treat directly in front of his nose.
4. Say the dog's name and the word "stand."
5. Lure the dog into a standing position by pulling the treat in a straight line, directly away from his nose.
6. As he reaches for the food, you may want to gently touch his belly to help him get into and remain standing.
7. Once your dog is standing, immediately praise him and offer the treat.
8. Repeat the exercise several times until your dog feels comfortable moving from a sit to a stand.

Stand: Stay

Now that your dog has learned the first element of the exercise, it is time to add the expectations to stay in that position while you stand up and move around her, including up to 6 feet away. If you have spent time working with your dog in heeling, when you first stand up next to your dog, she might immediately assume a sitting position, since sitting next to you will have become a habit. Patience and being proactive will be crucial at this stage of

Stand

Begin the "stand" exercise in the basic heel position.

Guide the dog into the standing position using your right hand on his collar and your left hand near the dog's loin area.

The stand can be one of the most challenging exercises to teach. When a dog makes the choice to relax and remain still, she will typically choose to sit or lie down. The stand presents an interesting dilemma: How do you explain to your dog that you expect him to remain standing and not walk away when standing is the position that most dogs assume when they are ready to walk off?

The final exercise requires that you move six steps in front of your dog.

Return to the heel position by walking to the right and behind your dog.

Move along only as quickly as your dog seems comfortable with the lessons. Avoid allowing him to move.

training. Your goal should be to prevent your dog from believing he has the opportunity to sit once you have instructed him to stand.

1. Say your dog's name and the command "stand" using the method described above.
2. Present a small treat if you would like, but do not let your dog move to eat it.
3. With your right hand, gently take control of her collar under the chin.
4. With your left hand, maintain a very light touch at her belly or loin area.
5. Tell her to stay and stand up, remaining in contact with her with both hands.

The judge at a trial may be male or female, tall or short, old or young. During training, try to find a variety of people to play the part of judge to familiarize your dog with the variety of people who might perform the "stand for examination" exercise at an obedience trial.

The scoring of the stand does not begin until the handler has given the command to stay. A dog that sits, lies down, moves away from the position in which it was left, growls, or shows resentment for the judge will receive a nonqualifying score.

6. Use your right fingers to gently massage her chest. Gently stroke her side or belly with your left hand. The point is to make your dog feel relaxed but also under your gentle control.

7. Once she has remained still for around thirty seconds, end the exercise.

8. Do not ask her to sit, but rather tell her to heel and walk forward a few feet.

9. Repeat the exercise until your dog becomes steady and you are able to remove your left hand.

10. Leave your right hand in her collar under her chin for a while longer as you increase the time you expect her to stay still.

11. Prevent any movement of her feet by going very slowly and maintaining contact as necessary.

12. With your right hand still under her chin to prevent any forward movement, use your left hand to begin an "examination." This should include gently petting her from head to tail and touching her legs and feet.

13. Release your two-handed touch and stand up next to your dog. If she shows any signs of moving, calmly replace your hands to reassure her of your expectations that she is to remain standing still.

14. Step in front of your dog and then circle around her back to heel position, helping her remain still.

15. Step 1 or 2 feet away from her. Increase the distance when your dog becomes more reliable while standing still.

16. Once you are able to stand 6 feet in front of your dog, you can play the role of judge, returning to her and touching her head.

Stand: Accept Examination

After your dog will remain still while you move about, examine her, and return behind her, it is time to expect her to remain still when a stranger examines her. Ask a reliable friend or family member to play the part of the judge. Go back to the beginning stages of the exercise by asking your dog to stand while you maintain two-handed contact with her collar and her belly area. The first exam should be a simple pat on the head by your assistant. Then the "judge" should step away. Reward your dog for remaining still. Practice until you can release your hands from your dog and the "judge" can pat her on the head. Maintain good vigilance so that you can catch her before she moves. Then ask the "judge" to touch her head and shoulders. Finally, have him touch the dog's head, shoulders, and rump. You should remain directly at your dog's side during the examination. The more patient and vigilant you are, the less likely your dog will move and the faster she will learn the exercise without making a mistake or developing the habit of sitting or walking away.

Not Just an Obedience Exercise

At a novice competition, the judge will touch only your dog's head, shoulders, and rump. But you may want to train your dog to accept a full examination from you. This will include looking into her ears and mouth. You should be able to touch any part of your dog's body, including her feet, belly, and tail, while she remains standing. Having trained your dog to accept such an exam will make your veterinarian very happy and allow for better health care in the event your dog requires medical attention.

Competition Recall

Refer to Chapter 5 to teach your dog the fundamental understanding of coming when called. Skills your dog should have prior to attempting the formal recall are a reliable sit from 30 feet away and an understanding of the basic recall command.

Formalizing the exercise to fit into the rules of the trial organization will require that you learn a few new tasks. In the lower levels of 4-H competitions, the recall exercise is performed on a 6-foot lead. Novice and higher-level AKC classes require that you leave your dog in a sit and move 30 feet away. Your dog must remain sitting until you call him under the direction of the judge.

In competition, the instructions you will receive from the judge are "leave your dog," "call your dog," and "finish." The exercise begins with the dog sitting in heel position.

Recall

The "recall" command begins with the dog sitting in heel position.

In the pre-novice class, the handler moves to the end of a 6-foot lead. In all other classes, the recall command is used off lead, and the handler moves to a position 30 feet from the dog.

Encouraging your dog to look up at you at the end of the recall can help him sit straight and centered. Points are deducted for a crooked sit.

Upon orders from the judge, the handler calls the dog.

The dog should sit squarely in front of the handler until the judge gives the order to "finish."

Creating an Attentive and Centered Dog during a Recall

To help a dog center on your body, dispense food rewards from a centered position. Use human-consumable treats, such as small pieces of a hot dog. Sit your dog directly in front of you. Place the treats in your mouth. Teach your dog to catch the treat as it falls from your mouth. This exercise will result in a dog that both centers on your body and looks up attentively when arriving after the recall command. Information on teaching a dog to catch food can be found in Chapter 8.

When the judge informs you to leave your dog, you are allowed to say his name and the word "stay." You may also pair a hand signal with your "stay" command. Then you must walk to a designated location about 30 feet away and turn and face your dog. You should hold your hands at your sides and make no additional hand or body gestures when you are told to call your dog.

Upon the judge's command, you will call your dog. You may use his name and your word for come. No other information may be given at that time. Do not bob your head, bend at the waist, or otherwise signal your dog beyond the verbal command. Your dog should come in a brisk trot or gallop and sit centered directly in front of you. He should not move until the judge instructs you to "finish." At that point, on your command, your dog should go smartly to the heel position. He may go around you to your right or swing around on your left side.

Teaching the Sit in Front

Because it truly doesn't matter during daily life, no emphasis was given in Chapter 5 to the position your dog should take when he arrives to you. As long as your dog doesn't believe he can race right past you or remain far enough from you that he engages in a game of catch-me-if-you-can, how he arrives when he is called is not important. However,

in a formal obedience competition, your dog must sit close enough that you could reach and touch him. You should also strive to teach him to sit centered in front of you. While the principle features of the exercise are a demonstration that your dog will sit and stay when you leave him and come promptly when called, you will lose valuable points if your dog does not sit in front of you or go to heel when told.

Because sitting perfectly is not a socially compliant sort of behavior, we teach it with the Incentive Method. Later, you may set a high standard for a straight front by employing the Comprehensive Method.

1. Sit your dog in heel position.
2. Swing around so that he is centered directly in front of you and you are standing toe to toe.
3. Step backward just one step.
4. Say your dog's name and the word "front" or "straight."
5. Step backward one or two steps (no more) to encourage him to come toward you.
6. Command him to sit.
7. Praise and reward him immediately.
8. Repeat several times, calling your dog to "front," instructing him to sit, then reminding him to stay, and stepping backwards a few feet.
9. Over time, step away farther and farther.

This method reduces the chance that your dog will sit crooked, since it limits the space in which to develop a crooked sit. It also gives your dog a word that signifies sitting centered and directly in front of you. Later, when you call your dog from a greater distance, if he is about to sit crooked, you can use the "front" command to remind him about proper front position. At the actual obedience trial, you will not be able to give the additional "front" command. But in the same way that during early heeling training we instruct the dog to sit when we come to a halt, helping the dog to "front" in the early stages of teaching a recall can develop a good habit and limit your dog from developing a crooked sit.

Teaching the Finish

Once your dog is sitting in front of you, he must get to the heel position so that you can walk away with him. That action is referred to as a finish. Because it is a nonsensical action from the dog's point of view, we will teach it as a trick using the Incentive Method. The main directive is to lure the dog from one position to another, then reward him for arriving. Breaking the exercise down to a few different components allows you to reward your dog along the way. That way he won't lose focus or initiative while waiting for a single reward at the very end.

Finish Right

In this exercise, the dog moves to your right, around behind you, and then up into proper heel position.

1. Sit your dog directly in front of you.
2. Put a treat in your right hand (you may also hold a lead in your right hand if you find it helpful).
3. Command your dog to "finish," "finish right," "heel," or "go around."

4. Using the treat positioned in front of his nose, lure him to the right side of your body (you may find that stepping backward with your right leg gives the dog additional helpful information).
5. Praise and reward him.
6. Repeat several times to create a dog that willingly gets up out of his sit and moves to the right side of your body.
7. Hold two treats in your right hand.
8. Follow the preceding steps and deliver a treat when your dog gets to your right side.
9. Continue luring the dog around behind your body using the second treat in your right hand.
10. Deliver the treat when the dog progresses to a point behind your body.
11. Repeat several times.
12. Put one treat in your right hand and one in your left hand (or use a food pouch strapped to your left side for easy access to treats).
13. Follow the preceding steps but eliminate the first food reward, delivering only the second treat when the dog is behind you.
14. Leaving the dog behind you, turn forward and reach back with your left hand to lure your dog into heel position.
15. Command him to sit.
16. Praise and reward him.
17. Repeat.
18. Diminish the frequency and number of food rewards as the dog demonstrates a confident understanding of the exercise.

The finish to the right is easier for larger dogs, since they have the whole trip around your back to straighten out and move back into proper heel position.

Finish Right

The "finish right" command begins with the dog sitting squarely in front of the handler.

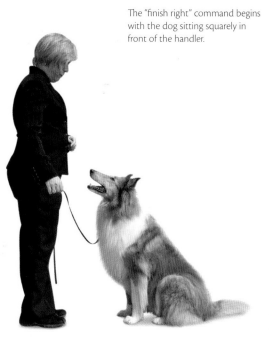

Step backward with your right leg.

Use a food lure to encourage the dog to move around your body.

Deliver the first food reward when the dog is behind you.

Transfer the lead from your right to your left hand.

Use a second food reward to lure the dog into the heel position.

Command the dog to sit.

Praise and reward the dog once he is sitting in the heel position.

Finish Left

Referred to as a swing or flip finish, the finish to the left side can be very challenging for long-bodied dogs or those that lack initiative.

Begin the "finish left" command with the dog sitting squarely in front of you. Hold the lead in your left hand.

Finish Left

In this exercise, the dog moves to your left, swings around, and then moves into proper heel position.

Step backward with your left leg while you present a food lure.

1. Sit your dog directly in front of you.
2. Put a treat in your left hand.
3. Give the command to "swing," "finish left," or "heel."
4. Step backward with your left foot and lure the dog to your left and directly backward.
5. Praise him and deliver the treat when he is facing opposite the direction you are facing.
6. Repeat.

94

Lure the dog to step straight backward, then deliver the reward.

Finish Left

Encourage your dog to turn into you and face forward using a food lure.

7. Once the dog is confidently getting up and moving backward, put two treats in your left hand.
8. Repeat the preceding steps. After delivering the first treat, lure your dog's head in toward your left leg.
9. Step forward with your left leg and lure the dog into the heel position with the second treat.

10. Give the command "sit" and deliver the second treat.
11. Repeat until the dog shows a keen desire to complete the behavior. Eliminate the first treat over time, then reduce the frequency of the second treat.

Step forward with your left leg to encourage your dog to move with you.

Lure the dog into the proper heel position.

Command your dog to sit, then praise and reward.

Competition Sit and Down

I believe that all dogs should be taught to sit or lie down and to stay put reliably, even in the presence of challenging distractions, such as squirrels, cats, other dogs, kids on skateboards, and loud noises. Apparently, the folks who created obedience competitions thought so as well. Out of the 200 possible points available in a novice obedience class, 60 points are dedicated to the sit and down exercises. While in heeling you may lose a number of points for a lag here or a sniff there, in the sit-stay you generally acquire all 30 points or lose all 30 points. In AKC

rules, which are used as guidelines for the 4-H program, there are 200 possible points. A competitor must earn no fewer than 170 points but also cannot lose more than 50 percent of the points in any exercise. Therefore, you may perform all the other exercises with great precision, but if your dog lies down during the one-minute sit exercise, you will not receive a qualifying score. Your dog must complete the sit and down-stay exercises or you will go home empty-handed.

While county-level 4-H classes may differ slightly from AKC rules, typically all dogs in the class are judged together, unless there is

Long Sit

The steps for performing the formal sit-stay at an obedience trial begin with the dog sitting in heel position.

Upon the judge's order to "leave your dog," handlers can tell their dogs to stay using verbal and hand signals.

Moving away from the dog, the handler is not permitted to utter any additional commands and must assume a position directly across from him.

The long sit in novice class lasts one minute. The handler should not fidget or otherwise move about during this time.

not sufficient room to provide for a 4-foot space between dogs. In that case, the class will be separated. You will be invited into the ring in the order in which you were judged individually. If you are in a class where the group exercises are performed off lead, you will be expected to remove the leash. If you are wearing a numbered armband, you will be asked to place it behind your dog, so that the judge can identify each dog.

When you are standing in a straight line, side by side with your fellow competitors, the judge will give the command to "sit your dog" or "down your dog," depending upon the exercise. You will be allowed to use your dog's name and a verbal command. You should not touch your dog or his collar. You should not position your dog with any force. Once all the dogs are in position and facing the other side of the ring, the judge will tell the class to "leave your dog." At that time, if you are in a class that is performed on a 6-foot lead, you will step to the end of your lead. In all higher classes, you will be expected to move across the ring—about 30 feet away—turn, and face your dog.

You may hold your hands at your side or crossed in front of you, but you should not fidget or otherwise move about. Any action on your part that could be considered giving the dog extra commands is not acceptable. In the novice class, the long sit exercise lasts for one minute. The long down is a three-minute exercise. In open class, the long sit lasts for three minutes while the handler is out of the dog's sight. The open long down requires the handler to remain out of the dog's sight for five very long minutes before being escorted back into the ring.

Once the time has elapsed, the judge will instruct the handlers to "return to your dog." All the handlers walk side by side back to the row of dogs. Each handler steps to the right to move behind his or her dog before stepping back into the heel position.

Long Sit

When the judge gives the command "return to your dog," the handler should move toward and to the right of the dog.

When walking behind the dog, the handler cannot touch or speak to the dog.

The exercise ends when handlers move back into heel position and the judge proclaims, "exercise finished." Until those words are spoken, handlers should not praise their dogs.

Down-Stay

During initial training, touching your dog's collar can be essential to setting expectations for behavior. But in competition, you will not be permitted to touch your dog.

The down-stay is similar to the sit-stay and also begins with the dog in heel position.

Training a toy dog can be an extra challenge. Many toy dogs have bold personalities. They are not interested in compliance and prefer to assume the position of king of the house. During early training, reinforcing standards for the down usually includes physical touch, which is not permitted in formal competition.

The novice down-stay lasts three minutes. It is typically the last exercise performed and therefore causes the most anxiety for 4-H moms and dads watching in the stands. If the dog has received a qualifying score for the other exercises, it can be heartbreaking if she gets up in this final exercise.

When first teaching a down-stay, step back and forth and around your dog to provide distractions. This early training will pay off well at the end of a formal down exercise.

Down-Stay

A dog must stay down until the judge says, "Exercise finished." Remaining calm and composed, and waiting a few extra seconds before praising your dog, will prepare him for the competition.

Group Sit

The group sit exercise is performed with handlers and dogs positioned about 4 feet apart. Dogs are not allowed to interfere with another dog's performance. A dog that does will be removed from the line and will be given a 0 for the exercise.

Competitors command their dogs to stay before being instructed to move away from their dogs.

Can Dogs Tell Time?

When practicing the long sit or long down exercise, refrain from using a stopwatch to end the exercise at exactly one or three minutes. Some dogs seem to present a keen sense of timing. If given the chance to learn the duration of an event, they might begin to fidget or end the exercise themselves when the expected time has elapsed. Practice performing a two- or three-minute-long sit exercise when preparing for the real event, which lasts only one minute. That way, you and your dog will feel confident in his ability to stay sitting for one minute.

During the group sit and down, very small movements or minimal whining can result in deductions. Most other infractions result in a 0 for the exercise. It is wise to train your dog in as many situations as possible.

When instructed by the judge to do so, competitors in a trial must command their dogs to lie down. You can use your dog's name once and give one verbal "down" command.

In the lower classes at a 4-H fair, handlers complete all the exercises, including the sit and down, on a 6-foot lead. In the novice class, handlers are required to move to the other side of the ring, which is 30 feet away.

ADDITIONAL TRAINING AND SKILLS

The first obedience class I entered was offered by a large dog training club. During the hours preceding and following my beginner class, the established members of the club worked their own dogs in intermediate and advanced level classes. As a first-time trainer, I was quite content with my own dog's accomplishments, but I wanted more. I wanted my dog to sail over a jump while retrieving a dumbbell. I wanted my dog to identify an article that contained my unique scent among a dozen others that did not. I made a point of arriving early and staying late in order to watch the club members labor through problems and celebrate their dogs' achievements. When my dog graduated from the beginner class, I promptly signed up for the next level. A few years later, while training my dog in an advanced class, I was approached by a beginner student. He asked whether I felt his dog could ever be as brilliant as mine. I told him that with work and patience, I was certain he would succeed.

This chapter offers a glimpse of the advanced level work that is required in the open and utility classes. It also provides detailed instruction on how to teach your dog to retrieve and discriminate scent on command. The four basic commands (sit, down, loose-lead walking, and come when called) are essential for success in advanced level work. However, once your dog has mastered the basics and behaves in a socially compliant manner, you may find it interesting to work on retrieving or scent discrimination while you are also perfecting competition level heeling. It can alleviate the stress that some dogs and handlers experience while preparing for their first trial.

Advanced Classes—Open and Utility

I strongly recommend securing a copy of the official rules that govern any event you want to enter. In the United States, the American Kennel Club sanctions more obedience events than any other organization. You can download obedience regulations from AKC's website. Another U.S. club that holds obedience trials is the United Kennel Club. Breed-specific clubs, such as the Australian Shepherd Club, provide obedience competitions that are often open to all breeds. Each organization has its own rules governing trials. 4-H events are usually held under AKC regulations.

Large Organizations That Sanction Obedience Trials in the United States

- American Kennel Club: www.akc.org
- United Kennel Club: www.ukcdogs.com
- Australian Shepherd Club: www.asca.org

To find an obedience club in your area, go to an Internet search engine and search for "obedience club" and your location.

The advanced classes that are offered by the AKC are open and utility. There are optional titling classes, which, for the purpose of providing more variety or an opportunity to secure additional titles, combine exercises from different classes. It is outside the scope of this book to offer detailed information for each open or utility exercise, but a creative use of the very thorough description of retrieving and scent discrimination, as well as the sample of tricks presented in Chapter 8, covers most of the skills necessary to compete in the advanced classes.

Open Class
Heel on Lead, Heel off Lead, Figure Eight off Lead

The big leap in skill required from novice to open is the introduction of heeling off lead. Using the "watch" command described in Chapter 6, along with setting standards around heel position using the Comprehensive Method, should provide all the information necessary to move from on lead to off lead, as long as you are dedicated to practicing. In my experience, moving from on to off lead is typically more of an issue for the handler than the dog. Once you are rarely or never using your lead to correct issues such as sniffing, forging ahead, or lack of attention, tuck it into your pocket or drape it over your neck. Relax and work your dog as if you were holding the lead. If you have followed the basic premises presented in the chapters about loose-lead walking and competitive heeling, getting to the state where you are no longer using the lead should be a fairly seamless event.

Drop on Recall

This exercise demonstrates your dog's ability to stop in mid-stride and assume a down position during a recall. In essence, it combines the standard recall with the "bang, you're dead" trick. I speculate that folks who struggle with teaching the "drop on recall" exercise have attempted to train the drop during the recall. While that is what the end product will be, teaching a dog to fall to the ground within the constructs of a recall is confusing at best.

This is a skill that should be broken down into separate parts that should not be combined until the dog is able to perform both elements with great enthusiasm and confidence.

While the "drop on recall" exercise seems highly complex, it is really a combination of several smaller, easier steps. Before a dog can learn to lie down when running, it needs to learn to lie down when standing.

When a dog assumes the down position, he can get a food reward. But over time, the food must be eliminated. Here, Kayleigh gives Snowbelle a hand signal to stay instead of a treat. This shifts the exercise to a more compliance-based approach.

1. Teach your dog to go down from a standing position (see "Bang, You're Dead" on page 160).

2. Work toward an immediate drop to a down from 1 then 2, 3, and 4 feet away, always reinforcing the expectation if necessary. (This can be done with a collar correction, which your dog will understand from the basic down training in Chapter 5.)

3. Once your dog can drop to a down position at 15 or 20 feet away, begin asking him to drop down when he is moving around. (Reinforce the expectation whenever necessary.)

4. Outside of the formal configuration of an official recall, call your dog from around 10 feet away. Give him the "down" command as he approaches you, so you can back it up if he fails to drop.

5. Work slowly backward toward a formal recall so that by the time you set up an official exercise, your dog is able and happy to drop when you command, regardless of the circumstances.

Retrieve on Flat and Retrieve over Jump and Broad Jump

Use the information in this chapter to prepare your dog for these open exercises. Jumping is described as a trick later in this chapter.

Long Sit and Down out of Sight

A socially compliant dog that recognizes your position as the authority figure develops loyalty and trust based on his social position. A socially balanced dog can handle his owner leaving now and again without becoming nervous or anxious. It is the dog that has an upside-down relationship with his person that will carry on and act out when left behind. Working at the very basic levels of sound discipline and practicing sit and down exercises in many locations and at varying distances, including stepping out of sight on occasion, should prepare you and your dog for the long sit and long down exercises found in the open class.

Utility Class Exercises
Signal Exercises

The heeling pattern in utility class adds a few additional components that are not found in heeling in open and novice class. First, the handler is not allowed to give voice commands but must instead use hand signals. Replacing voice commands with hand

Enthusiasm Defines Confidence

Most people want their dogs to appear, and in fact, be happy when working. However, some people make the mistake of attempting to teach a dog to be happy. A confident dog will be happy. It is best to teach with the goal of creating a confident partner and to know that happiness will happen. Learning is stressful. To expect your dog to appear relaxed and carefree when learning something new is to lack sensitivity. Just because your dog doesn't appear happy during initial training does not imply that you need to change your methods to help the dog appear happy all the time. Your goal should be to provide instruction that is clear, concise, and broken down into digestible pieces that your dog can conquer. Work toward creating a self-assured dog and you will develop a happy dog. Happy, confident dogs are more likely to perform their tasks with speed and enthusiasm.

The AKC open class includes two exercises that require a dog to retrieve a dumbbell to hand: the "retrieve on flat" and the "retrieve over high jump" exercises. In both exercises, a dog that fails to leave the handler on the first command to fetch the dumbbell receives a 0.

The dog is required to go directly to the dumbbell, return promptly, and deliver it to hand without dropping it.

The skills that a dog learns in earlier exercises, such as sitting squarely in front of the handler and performing a finish after the recall, are also required in these exercises.

signals is not terribly difficult for most dogs to understand. As a species, dogs prefer to "listen" to body language rather than vocal commands anyway.

At some point during the normal pace heeling, the judge signals to the handler to "stand your dog." Then the judge will instruct the handler to "leave your dog." The handler must communicate the stand and the stay with hand signals and may not use any voice commands. The signal exercise is a means of demonstrating that the dog can perform a sit, down, and recall under hand signals alone. The judge may not use audible instructions to command the handler to first sit, then down, and then recall the dog.

Teaching your dog to obey hand signals is quite simple. Once the dog has learned an exercise with verbal commands, you need only pair a hand signal with the verbal command and back up any lack of compliance to educate your dog on the new form of communication.

Scent Discrimination

See page 127.

Directed Retrieve

The principle components of this exercise are to demonstrate the dog will remain sitting until sent to retrieve and will retrieve the specific article (one of three that are presented) to hand. See later in this chapter for a thorough description of retrieving. The idea of directing the dog to a specific article pairs the concept of obeying signals with retrieving. Three primarily white utility gloves are provided by the competitor. They are placed across the end of ring, equidistant from each other. The judge designates to the handler, who is facing with the dog away from the gloves, which glove is to be fetched.

Teaching a dog to follow the line presented by your arm or hand involves creating a clear signal for your dog and limiting errors that may set a habit of haphazard selection. I have been successful in using a technique that emulates the concept of a hunter and his gun to send a dog on a blind retrieve. The handler is allowed to bend as low as necessary to provide a signal with her left arm in the direction of the glove she expects the dog to retrieve. Holding my left elbow at my waist and extending my forearm straight out from my body with finger tips pointing at the glove before sending the dog with a verbal retrieve command is usually plenty of information for a dog to hone in on a specific glove. In early training, limiting the number to just one glove is prudent. Then, adding the distraction of a second glove, which is placed a significant distance from the first glove, sets up the dog for success. Moving the second glove closer to the position it will be during the trial and adding the third glove slowly over time creates a reliable directed retrieve.

Moving Stand

This exercise combines a thorough examination by the judge with a moving halt, while the handler continues walking. Whereas in most other elements in competition the handler and dog come to a stop at the same time, in the moving stand exercise the dog is expected to halt instantaneously in a standing position while the handler continues forward for about 10 feet, then turns and faces the dog. Then the judge performs a more meticulous exam than is found in the novice-level "stand for examination." Finally, the dog is called directly to heel position instead of first stopping in front of the handler, as is customary in all other maneuvers where the dog is at a remote location at some point in the exercise.

The moving stand is the perfect place to employ the Comprehensive Method, since high standards must be set and boundaries for the dog's actions need to be clearly defined. Start by using the Incentive Method to shape the primary components of the exercise. Then, if necessary, set strict limits for the dog's movement and position using collar corrections that are sufficient to set expectations for behavior.

Directed Jumping

Envision a baseball diamond. The directed jumping exercise asks your dog to travel from home plate to second base and then to jump over an obstacle found at first or third base. This exercise requires a dog to leave her handler's side and run off in a straight line to the other end of the ring. When instructed to do so, the dog sits and faces her handler. The judge tells the handler whether to send the dog to the high jump (made of solid material) or the bar jump (a single bar). Upon completing the jump, the dog returns to the handler in much the same way as she did in the recall exercise. Then the dog is sent a

The moving stand gives a handler the opportunity to use a variety of training methods. The initial stand position can be lured. Physically placing or holding the dog in the stand position until he understands that he is expected to stay put is also useful. Finally, you can set high standards using the Comprehensive Method.

second time to execute the second type of jump.

The use of a bridge to mark desired behaviors with the Incentive Method is truly designed for this type of exercise. When your dog is in a remote location, having the capacity to tell her that she is correct is invaluable. Providing a target to which the dog can move is to your advantage. When there is good communication, directed jumping is fun for the dog and the handler. Developing great communication through the use of a target and rewarding desired actions are key to achieving success.

This is also an exercise that should be broken down into its smallest components. Running out in a straight line is a unique task, regardless of whether jumping is involved or not. First start teaching your dog to move out to a target and sit on command. Limiting the available jumps to just one will give your dog a chance to succeed and to learn about your directed signals (left arm out means the dog should take the jump on your left). Shortening the distances and bringing the jumps closer together in the beginning will allow you to be up close and personal when helping your dog understand your directions.

Teaching the Retrieve

Back in my early dog-training days in Chicago, I used to park my car in a church lot behind my apartment. After work, I often took my dogs there and practiced obedience, setting up jumps and inviting neighborhood kids to participate in my dogs' training. While it was helpful in some ways that my Labrador retriever was born to fetch, I never knew how valuable it was until one day in May. I was unable to find my wristwatch just before leaving for work. I left for the office without it.

After work, I took my dogs to the church lot to practice and then play a bit of fetch. The rain from the previous evening had created deep puddles, but as a water dog, Stella didn't mind. I threw the ball and she brought it back. Again and again, I tossed and she fetched. She was an insatiable retriever. Then, as she was running back to me with the soggy tennis ball, she stopped dead in her tracks next to a deep puddle. Dropping the ball, she stuck her nose into the dark water and began running back to me. She had left the ball behind, and I was stunned. She never failed to bring her ball. As she got closer, I noticed that she had something in her mouth. She arrived, sat directly in front of me, and held the object up for me to take. It was my wristwatch!

On page 127, I will present information on how to teach your dog to discriminate scent on command. In many odor discrimination scenarios, the ability to detect and distinguish scents is fairly useless if your dog cannot fetch an object that she has identified with her keen sense of smell.

Any dog can be taught to retrieve objects on command. While some breeds have a natural, genetically driven drive to fetch, others do not. You might think it's easy to teach a natural retriever to fetch, but that depends on the standard you are seeking. Using a dog's natural prey or fetch drive leaves too much control over when and if to retrieve

to the dog. This can become frustrating if you expect a dog to retrieve on command and deliver to your hand any object, even one that she doesn't particularly like.

The technique described below is very methodical. It assumes that the dog has little or no desire to race after objects and bring them back. It does not rely on—in fact it avoids—any natural tendency for the dog to retrieve. It provides clear, concise information to the dog about your expectations to take, pick up, and finally retrieve any object you choose.

Time for a Reminder
If you are using a bridge word or clicker, present the bridge as soon as your dog displays the desired behavior and immediately preceding the reward.

Precursor behaviors that are invaluable to teaching the retrieve are sit and come. Entering into retrieving training with a substandard sit or recall can make the exercise very challenging.

Take your time teaching this exercise. Your patience will be rewarded. Stay relaxed. Start with a single object for retrieving. This can be a dish towel that has been rolled and taped into a long cylinder, a wooden dowel, an obedience dumbbell, or any other object that seems to fit well into your dog's mouth.

There are four components to retrieving:

1. Take it.
2. Hold it.
3. Give it.
4. Fetch it.

While you might think that fetching is the most important behavior and should come first in the training process, we will teach the

This service dog has been taught to fetch, hold, and deliver to hand any object that her partner may require. Whether she is asked to pick up a fallen credit card or this large pitcher, Bree can assist her disabled handler because she has been taught to retrieve.

dog to take, hold, and give the object before we ever toss it. That groundwork needs to be in place before you can ask a dog to perform at a remote distance.

Take It and Hold

While no time limit should be arbitrarily placed on teaching any exercise, if you work about five to ten minutes per day in a calm, relaxed, and persistent manner, by the end of a week, your dog should be able to take and hold an object. Although it may seem

like you are expecting very little in the first couple of days, many dogs need a day or so to absorb your expectations. It is not uncommon that, initially, a dog seems utterly resistant to allowing a strange object to make contact with his tongue. Twenty-four hours later, on the first or second command, your dog may act as though he has been taking and holding the object for months. However, a dog that senses frustration, anxiety, or anger from his handler may shut down his ability to learn. Remain tolerant to your dog's learning schedule.

Lisette presents a dumbbell to Adair and hopes he will move a bit forward to investigate it.

Any sign of interest is rewarded with food.

Day 1

1. Begin with your dog sitting in front of you. Use a lead to keep him close if necessary.
2. While holding a high-value treat in one hand, present the object with your other hand.
3. Tell the dog "take it" in a happy tone.
4. Reward *any* movement toward the object, even if it's only to sniff it.
5. Remain calm and repeat several times.
6. At some point, your dog will probably make contact with the object, even if by accident. Reward that contact instantly. Give a windfall of treats and carry on about what a super dog he is.
7. End the initial training session when the dog moves toward the object and touches it. Wait twenty-four hours before the next session.

Day 2

1. Begin again with the dog sitting in front of you.
2. Repeat the exercise from the previous day, but limit the bridge or reward to times when the dog reaches out toward the object. If your dog was trained to "touch it" earlier, he may think this is a "touch it" exercise and show at least that much interest in the object.
3. If the dog makes any move to open his mouth to take the object or check it out with his teeth, reward him with a windfall of treats and high praise. Wait another twenty-four hours before doing this exercise again.

Day 3

1. On day 3, if the dog has not shown any desire to touch or open his mouth to take the object, it is time to help him understand your expectations.
2. Gently take his muzzle in your hand.
3. Use your thumb and fingers to kindly open his jaws.

4. Touch his tongue with the object.
5. Immediately bridge, praise, and reward.
6. Repeat several times.
7. The expectation for day 3 is that the dog tolerates the object on his tongue because he will receive a great reward.
8. Wait another twenty-four hours before working this exercise.

Day 4

1. The dog should be actively opening his mouth when the object is presented, if only to allow it to touch his tongue. Many dogs will begin grabbing for the object at this time in anticipation of a food reward.
2. If the dog is not grabbing for the object yet, continue to open his mouth. This time, place it into his mouth rather than just touching it to his tongue.
3. Making certain that the object sits comfortably just behind his canine teeth, gently squeeze his muzzle shut over the object with a very light touch (with one finger over the bridge of his nose and your thumb under his chin) and say "hold."

If a dog does not reach for the dumbbell, even after a few days of introduction, the handler should open his mouth and place the dumbbell in it. If at some later point in the training process the dog resists taking the dumbbell, the handler can go back to this very basic step. A dog's refusal can be frustrating for the handler; remaining calm and methodical is the key to moving beyond this point. Going back to an early step can help the dog overcome his stubbornness.

4. Immediately say "give," then take the object from his mouth. Always keep one hand on the object so that it never falls to the ground.

5. Reward and praise him immediately.

6. For some dogs, this is an aha moment, when they realize that all you want is for them to take and hold the object. Some dogs will begin to clamp down on the object at this time.

7. Repeat the take it, hold, and give scenario, with immediate rewards, ten to fifteen times.

8. Wait twenty-four hours before the next training session.

Day 5

1. Release your gentle grasp on the muzzle for a second to see if your dog is clamping his own mouth shut or if it is your pressure that is keeping the object in his mouth.

2. If he is clamping on the object at the "hold" command, wait a second before commanding him to "give."

3. Take the object and reward him immediately.

Day 6 and Beyond

1. Have the dog hold the object for longer periods before asking him to give.

2. On the "take it" command, expect more and more of your dog. Instead of presenting the object directly in front of him, hold it off to one side or the other. Move the object higher or lower than his muzzle when you tell him to take it. Move the object very close to the ground or set it atop a chin-high table. He should begin to move toward the object to grab it from you at this stage.

To encourage the dog to hold and clamp down on the dumbbell, Lisette gently applies pressure with a finger and thumb while saying "hold."

When removing the dumbbell from the dog's mouth, say "give" and immediately reward the dog.

Once the dog is taking and holding the dumbbell, remove your grasp for a very short time. Then tell the dog "give" before he chooses to drop the dumbbell.

While it is more comfortable to teach the retrieve from a sitting position, once your dog can perform the take it, hold, and give, it's time for you to stand up and expect the same from your dog. Many dogs struggle a bit with this shift in your position, but they recover quickly and transfer their earlier lessons to the new situation.

Stand up and repeat all the basic steps that you performed while sitting. These include gently holding your dog's muzzle shut around the dumbbell before letting go. If you keep the dumbbell from dropping to the ground, you won't have to address that training issue later. Teaching a dog is about creating a good habit without allowing unacceptable behaviors.

Fetching

Once your dog is grabbing for the object in your hand, regardless of where you hold it, it is time to slowly move it to the floor. When you first place it on the ground, keep your hand on the object so the dog's experience is only slightly different than it was when you moved it right, left, up, and down. When you finally place the object on the floor and remove your hand, expect your dog to act as if she doesn't understand what you are asking. Some dogs do not know they can pick

If you look or point at the dumbbell, the dog is apt to focus on it too. Research has shown that dogs are more likely to follow a human's gaze than tame wolves, dogs' closest relatives. Take advantage of this trait in your training by focusing on tasks you expect your dog to perform.

ADDITIONAL TRAINING AND SKILLS

123

If you are using a bridge-and-reward technique, at the moment your dog reaches for the dumbbell on the ground, offer the bridge and then allow the dog to complete the remainder of the task. In this case, Adair will hear the bridge for taking the dumbbell in his mouth but will not receive the reward until he has completed the retrieve by sitting in front of his handler and relinquishing the object upon the "give" command.

Here, the handler claps her approval for a job well done. Rewards should have value related to the difficulty of the task. The first time a dog accomplishes a difficult job, the reward should be significantly higher than that given for simple skills.

the object up off the floor and hold it if you are not also holding it. You need to help her understand. Here is a point in training where your patience will be highly rewarded.

1. Put the object on the ground.
2. Tell your dog "take it."
3. Stand up.
4. Remain calm, relaxed, and patient.
5. If your dog stands perplexed, remain quiet and maintain a gaze directly at the object on the ground.
6. Once your dog picks up the object, tell her to hold, give, and take it.
7. Praise and reward her.

If your dog cannot grasp the idea of picking up the object from the floor if you are not holding one end, keep holding it for another few days, then try again.

Now that your dog is able to pick the object up off the floor and hold it until you take it from him on the "give" command, you can add a bit of distance to create the actual retrieve. This is where a reliable sit and recall come in handy.

Some dogs seem very perplexed by the requirement to carry the object. It's worth breaking the exercise down into a sequence of small steps.

1. Sit your dog.
2. Have him take the object and hold it.
3. Step backward about 2 feet.
4. Call your dog using the "come" command.
5. Expect your dog to drop the object and come to you. Do not get frustrated or angry if he drops the object.
6. If your dog comes toward you holding the object, instruct him to sit.
7. Expect your dog to drop the object; many dogs do. Do not get frustrated or angry if he does drop the object.
8. Tell your dog "give" and take the object from him.
9. Praise and reward him.

Quirky Moments in Training the Retrieve

Oddly, some dogs are perplexed about:

- Sitting from a standing position while holding a dumbbell. Most dogs will drop the dumbbell when asked to sit for the first time.
- Picking a dumbbell off the floor once the handler is no longer touching it.
- Walking and holding a dumbbell at the same time.
- Performing the take it when the handler moves from a sitting position to a standing position or vice versa.
- Taking, holding, and retrieving an object other than the one she first learned to retrieve.

These odd reactions are the reason this method has so many tiny steps. Any time your dog does not perform the task you are asking, you need only go back one small step to reach a point where she was successful.

Do not move forward into the process until the dog can perform the previous skill. If the dog appears confused with a new element, go backward one step to rebuild her confidence.

If your dog dropped the object either when you called him or when he attempted to sit in front of you, do not fret.

1. Set up the situation again.
2. Before you instruct the dog to come, gently put your thumb and finger over his muzzle as you did when teaching him to hold.
3. While maintaining slight pressure on the muzzle, command your dog to come and hold.
4. Step backward no more than one or two steps.
5. Instruct him to sit and hold while maintaining gentle pressure on his muzzle with your thumb and finger.
6. Repeat this exercise in the same way you trained your dog to "hold it" while sitting in front of you. Since he has been exposed to that step of the exercise before, it will be easier for him to understand your expectations.
7. Practice the primary steps of the "take it" (object placed on the floor), "hold," "come" (while you step backward and the dog comes toward you), "sit and hold," and "give" commands.
8. Add about 1 foot of distance each day for a week. At the end of a week, your dog should be able to pick up the object, come about 6 to 10 feet, and sit in front of you with a high level of reliability.

Until your dog can pick up an object that you place on the floor, bring it a few feet to you, and then sit to deliver it, you should not toss the object. Tossing the object should be the last step in the process of retrieving. The first time you toss the object, do so after practicing the above exercise a few times. Toss it about 2 or 3 feet away and command your dog to "take it," "hold" (if you still need that word as encouragement), "come," and "sit."

Because it will have become a habit for your dog to pick up the object, and because you will toss it only a few feet, your dog will more than likely go and pick it up for you. Then you should celebrate!

If your dog doesn't immediately retrieve, remember to remain calm and patient. Allow your dog to think about what you just said. Keep your gaze on the object. If he entirely loses interest, slowly move toward the object and reach for it. Tell your dog to take it. At that stage it will appear so much like what he has been practicing and what has resulted in a reward for his efforts, he will reach and pick up the object.

Time for a Reminder

When using the Incentive Method to create desired behaviors, as the dog starts to perform a task close to 80 percent of the time, begin to diminish the delivery of rewards. Remember to give the rewards in a random pattern.

Once your dog can retrieve the initial object to hand at a high level of success, you may begin to add new objects. When introducing the first five or so new objects, go back to square one (do not skip a step). Moving from a hard, solid object, such as a plastic dumbbell, to a soft or plush object is a unique challenge for some dogs. Moving to smaller objects, such as writing pens, can also unnerve some dogs. Always begin back at the very first "take it for a treat while sitting in front of me" step of the process. Your dog will move forward in the process very quickly if his initial training went smoothly and if he fully understands the concept.

Scent Discrimination

I was around nine years old when my family acquired our first puppy, a miniature schnauzer named Caesar. I recall teaching him several fun tricks. One was hide and seek. With practice, my sisters and I were able to make Caesar stay sitting in the living room while we went off and hid around the house. Then, from our remote hideouts, we would call Caesar to come find us, which he did with great enthusiasm and speed. It became quite a challenge to find a hiding place that truly tested his impressive ability. I recall the bathtub, behind the shower curtain, as being a bit more difficult than most other locations. As a child, I thought this was because he could not see me. In fact, it was probably more due to the way the tub held in my scent.

We also had great fun tossing a small river rock into a sea of thousands of others and watching as Caesar searched out the very stone we threw and brought it back to us. Each rock had a unique pattern of tiny fossils or colors, which made it possible for us to determine whether he was fetching the one we had actually tossed. But even without those cues, it was obvious by the way he worked his nose among the rocks that he was on a mission to search out the one containing our scent.

To find us and to locate a specific stone among thousands of others, Caesar used his keen sense of smell, paired with his desire to perform a job for us. All dogs have the capacity not only to detect very small amounts of scent but also to distinguish similar but unique scents from each other. In the same way we can detect subtle differences in color with our eyes, dogs can detect very slight differences in scent with their noses. As we drive past a corn field in summer, racing by at 50 miles per hour, we are still able to identify specific leaves on the corn plant Tassels, ears, bent and broken leaves, crooked stalks, the light yellow edges highlighted by the sun, and the deep green and almost black depths where leaves connect to stems are all discernible to our naked eyes. We see it all, process it immediately, and know what we are experiencing. I believe a dog's sense of smell is as accurate at taking in and processing both the gross and most delicate of scent information as we see all the hues of green in a cornfield.

With that understanding of a dog's ability to discriminate among odors, we can employ our dogs to carry out very sophisticated tasks or teach them to perform entertaining tricks. Hunters have long used dogs' ability to trail scent for food and sport. Bird dogs point, flush, and retrieve game most often using their exceptional sense of smell as their primary tool. Hounds trail small game such as rabbits, raccoons, and foxes, as well as big predators such as bears, cougars, and lions. Some breeds have been designed to hunt very specific species.

Search and rescue (SAR) dogs work with their handlers to accomplish a variety of duties using different scenting skills. Some dogs are trained to follow a very specific trail, such as a lost child or a criminal who has left the scene of a crime. Often these dogs are provided an object that contains the scent of the person or are taken to an exact location where the person was last seen. Some SAR dogs are trained to air scent and locate any person in a specific area. These dogs may work at disaster scenes, searching for victims lost in the rubble of an earthquake. Other SAR dogs are trained to find the remains of a cadaver, either on land or even in water.

A dog's keen sense of smell can be focused on a specific item or group of items to provide exceptional assistance to law enforcement personnel or other organizations. Some dogs are trained to sniff for fruit or meats illegally brought into a country at borders or airports.

This is John and his dog Sara. Sara is a ten-month-old border collie bred by the author. Sara is learning the tasks of a certified avalanche search and rescue dog. To train these dogs, handlers begin with a simple game of hide and seek. They progress to hiding "victims" in shallow, open cavities in the snow. Finally, they create an L-shaped tunnel that contains a small snow cave at the bottom. The "victim" crawls to the bottom of the cave, and the rest of the team turns over the top layer of snow to eliminate any visual cues. A certified dog must be able to find two victims buried at least 3 feet down in a 150-by-150-foot area in twenty minutes. Sara has achieved that goal in just ninety seconds! *James Coulter*

Others are trained to detect illegal narcotics. Dogs can even be trained to sniff out termites hidden in difficult-to-access rafters or foundations of homes.

Detecting cancer or other abnormal shifts in a person's biochemistry has become a new use for our beloved canines' desire to work for us using their incredible sniffers. Some service dogs are trained to detect drops in blood sugar for people with diabetes. Other dogs alert sick people that scheduled medications are required. It is all or in part dogs' keen sense of smell that allows them to provide these life-altering and sometimes lifesaving services.

Teaching your dog to use his natural scent discrimination abilities towards tricks and entertainment or as a means of developing an exceptional working bond with your dog is quite easy to do. All dogs follow scent trails, and all dogs make distinctions between people, animals, and objects via scent. Therefore, we don't need to teach the dog to sniff, but just sniff for us. Wondering whether dogs enjoy sniffing is like asking a person if she enjoys seeing things. It is a natural aspect of a dog's essence to use scent to make judgments and decisions about where to go and why.

The top level of competitive obedience requires a scent discrimination exercise. The handler brings to the trial five articles each made of leather, metal, and, in some organizations, wood. Before the exercise begins, a stranger (the judge or ring steward) touches eight articles (metal, leather, or wood) to infuse them with scent. They are then positioned on the ground about 20 feet away from the handler and dog and about 6 inches apart from each other. The handler impregnates an article with his or her own scent. While the dog and handler look away, the article is placed amongst the others using a method that avoids adding the judge's scent. Upon being commanded to turn around and face the pile of articles, the dog is sent to retrieve only the object that was handled by her owner. The exercise is repeated with the other article. The dog may sniff around the pile for a reasonable amount of time, but then must come back with the article that was scented by her owner and deliver it to hand.

The scent discrimination competition is the formal version of a trick you can train your dog to perform that will leave your friends in awe. Consider replacing the leather or metal articles with paper money. Ask your friends to crumple (so they are easy to pick

Each dog has a unique style of performing the scent discrimination exercise. Some are so confident in their abilities that they race out to the pile of articles, pick up the appropriate one, and return to their handlers without seeming to have spent any time making the determination. Other dogs move methodically from one object to the next, taking time to inhale an object's scent before moving on. They may move beyond the correct object to smell the others, with the goal of being absolutely certain of their decision. As long as a dog remains in a working mode, style differences are not penalized during official competitions.

up) a few one-dollar bills and place them in a pile on the floor. Inform your friends that your dog understands the value of money. Then take out a ten-dollar bill, crumple it, and slyly infuse it with your scent while doing so. Put your dog on a sit or down, facing away from the pile of money, letting folks know that you don't want him to peek. Then place the

ten-dollar bill among the other bills. Moving back to your dog, tell your friends that your dog finds value in bringing back only big bills. Send him to retrieve the ten-dollar bill, which he will do promptly, having been trained to fetch only articles that contain your scent. Your friends will be amazed and will pat you on the back for having such a marvelous pup.

Managing Scent Articles

Like my dog Stella, who brought back my wristwatch after it sat in a rain puddle for more than twenty-four hours, dogs can detect a specific scent days after it was left at a scene or on an object. For that reason, when working your dog on scent tasks, it is important to properly manage articles to avoid confusing your dog. If you choose to use several identical articles during training, you should mark each one with a unique number. On the first day of training, place your scent on article 1 and ask a friend to apply his or her scent to the others. At the end of the training session, touch every article to normalize your scent on all of them. Keep the items in a container that allows air to flow through it so that over time your scent will dissipate. The next training day, use article 2 and have someone else touch the others. At the end of the session, again touch all the articles to normalize your scent across all the objects. In this way, regardless of how often you use the articles, and regardless of whether your dog can detect your old scent on the objects, he will learn to detect the "hot," or most current, scent during the exercise. If you do not have a helper to touch the other articles during training, your dog will still be able to fetch the one you most recently handled because he will understand that he is to find the "hot" item.

Like my childhood pet Caesar, many dogs prefer to fetch items that contain their owners' scent. Therefore, teaching a dog to discriminate between your scent and another person's can be quite easy. One method employs the use of an incentive to first draw the dog to the appropriate object and then to help him make the mental pairing between your scent and an enjoyable experience. Using a product like a canned, squirt cheese, you can put a small dab of delicious food onto the article you wish your dog to discriminate from the other item that does not contain the cheese. Because dogs continually use their sense of smell, if the item containing cheese also contains your scent and the item without the cheese does not, he will learn to recognize the difference.

Here is a human example that may help explain the phenomenon. Place a cookie on a red placemat and nothing on a blue placemat that sits beside it on a table. Tell a child to go get the cookie. Repeat this exercise every day. Always put the cookie on the red placemat, but sometimes put the red placemat on the

left side of the table and sometimes on the right. Within a few days, the child will no longer pan across the mats to spot the cookie. He or she will go directly to the red placemat for the treat. Without additional guidance or instruction, the child's brain will make the association between the color red and the cookie. This association takes place at a level of brain functioning that does not require reason or sophisticated teaching.

Dogs use their sense of smell like we use our eyes, so by placing a little dab of cheese on an article that contains "hot" scent, the dog's brain makes the association without further information. Once the amount of cheese is reduced and then removed entirely, when you say "find mine," the dog will reliably fetch the article with your scent and leave behind those without it.

Some dogs are so interested in bringing back the article that they focus more on retrieving than scenting. Those dogs may require some additional information about your expectations. One method is to use a base made of vinyl matting or peg board.

The article that is not scented (or is scented by a stranger) is secured to the mat or board with a piece of light string or fishing line. The scented article (with or without food incentive) is then placed next to the tethered object and the dog is sent to retrieve the scented article. If he chooses the wrong one, he will not be able to bring it back, since it is attached to the base. His next option is the correct article, which he will be lavishly praised for fetching.

Step-by-Step Scent Discrimination: Discerning One Article from Another Based on "Hot" Scent

Valuable precursor skills for this exercise include retrieving to hand. Necessary tools include two of the same item (leather, metal, or wood, for example) that your dog has been trained to retrieve at a high level of reliability. Label the items 1 and 2.

1. Apply scent to both articles.
2. Let them sit untouched for about twenty-four hours.
3. Sit your dog and expect a solid stay.
4. Using a pair of tongs to avoid contaminating it with your scent, move article 2 about 10 feet away from you and your dog.
5. Apply scent to article 1 by holding it in your hand and rubbing it gently in your palms.
6. Apply a small amount of a soft, spreadable food treat, such as canned squirt cheese, cream cheese, or liverwurst, onto article 1. The dab of food should be no larger than the eraser on a pencil.
7. Set article 1 about 1 foot away from article 2. Article 1 should be the first article your dog encounters.
8. Return to your dog.
9. Give the command to fetch (such as "find mine") and send your dog to retrieve the

Traditional articles are single- or double-bar dumbbells made of leather or metal. However, some competitors get creative and use objects such as metal cups from a child's tea set or infant shoes made of leather. Showing creativity during competitions can lighten up the atmosphere, which can become quite stiff at times. In early training, adding a dab of soft cheese spread to the "hot" scented article can help a dog learn the task.

article. Expect him to lick the cheese off the article before taking further action.

10. If he returns with article 1, praise him profusely and reward him.

11. If he returns with article 2, stand completely still. Do not reach to take the article. Some dogs will then go back and fetch the other article.

12. If he returns with article 2 and shows no interest in completing the exercise, use a tie-down board from this point forward.

13. Repeat several times.

14. As reliability increases, begin moving the scented article in different positions relative to the unscented article. Use the position behind the unscented article as the last configuration. This is intended to help your dog be successful.

15. Once your dog shows a keen ability to fetch the scented article, add a second, third, and fourth unscented article slowly over time.

The concept of selecting the object that contains your scent can be applied to any number of creative tricks. You can fool your audience into believing that your dog can read or differentiate colors or shapes by slyly applying your odor to the article that you want your dog to identify while having volunteers handle the other objects.

If you are very enthusiastic about the idea of working your dog in serious scent discrimination activities, you may want to visit with a search and rescue group to ask questions about what it takes to become a certified canine handler. Don't be surprised if you are told it can take years to both train a dog and sufficiently learn about the job to become reliable enough to be deployed on an actual search. The best way to gain knowledge is to volunteer to help with activities such as laying tracks for other handlers, carrying water for the working search dogs during practice missions, or keeping records.

Rally Obedience

The 4-H obedience program is based on the standard AKC obedience classes: novice, open, and utility. Since January 2005, the AKC has been offering licensed clubs the option to host rally obedience trials. Rally is a fun, fast-paced, ever-changing event comprised of ten to twenty exercises that are set along a course in the fashion of an agility trial. The handler moves from one station to the next, performing each exercise. A judge does not call out commands but does oversee the team's work. Scores are based on precision at executing each element as well as time required to complete the course.

Unlike traditional obedience trials, the handler is permitted to speak to his or her dog throughout the course. Originally promoted as a stepping stone between the Canine Good Citizen Program and competitive novice obedience, rally has become a popular dog-training sport. At some point in the future, 4-H may offer a rally event. In the meantime, you can join a local dog club to learn more about it and practice with others. It is an excellent way to hone skills and develop a tight bond with your dog.

Trick Training

Teaching your dog to perform tricks is a highly valuable endeavor. It develops a strong bond, teaches your dog to focus on you, increases your dog's vocabulary, and develops his mind. Trick training can also be an excellent way to keep him physically limber and agile. The list of tricks you can teach your dog is virtually endless.

The formal obedience exercises found in competition trials are based on essential required commands that any dog should understand. While they can be taught as tricks using the Incentive Method alone, the canine mind understands the concept of obedience to an authority figure. The basic commands tend to emulate behaviors a dog might be expected to perform as a member of a well-balanced social canine pack. While the Incentive Method was used to introduce most of those commands, the Comprehensive Method was suggested to establish a high standard of performance. The Comprehensive Method emulates natural canine communication of setting a boundary and reinforcing it by providing prompt feedback, in the way of a correction, for noncompliance.

On the contrary, training a dog to perform tricks usually has little to do with obedience to authority or absolute compliance. The activity is fun, engaging, and entertaining for both dog and handler. The expectation of perfection is rarely considered a goal when teaching a dog to perform most tricks. It is a way to enjoy the extraordinary canine-human relationship. Therefore, for the most part, the method used in this section will be purely incentive.

Shake Paw

While it is often one of the most common tricks folks tend to teach their pets, many people do not recognize its value as a precursor behavior to many other skills. If you would like to teach your dog to wave, turn off a light, or push shut a cabinet door, shake paw is the right starting point.

When it comes to learning how to shake paw, dogs tend to fall into one of two categories. Hand-oriented dogs will present their paws early on to solve problems. Other dogs must be coaxed and coached to use their paws to achieve a goal. Dogs in the latter category often excel at using their mouths to

manipulate their world. Mouth-motivated dogs may be exceptional at retrieving. Paw-motivated dogs might already use their feet to pull open crate doors or hold toys while lying upside down. I describe two methods to teach shake paw. Choose the one that best serves your individual dog.

It's important to note that a dog will be less likely to learn if her handler manipulates her body into desired positions rather than coaching her to perform the behavior under her own skeletal-muscle control. When teaching shake paw, you will have less success by reaching down and picking up your dog's paw than if you use a method that helps her to perform the movement on her own.

Shake Paw Method 1:
The Paw-Oriented Dog

1. Begin with your dog sitting in front of you. If necessary, wrap a lead around your leg to keep him close. Remember the lead should never be tight.

2. In your right hand, hold a high-value treat inside your closed fingertips so that the dog can smell it, and perhaps even taste it by licking through your fingers, but cannot actually reach it to acquire it.

3. Present your hand at the dog's nose level.

4. In a happy tone of voice, as if to say "Do you want it?" give the command "shake,"

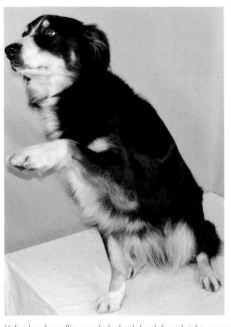

Yoli, a border collie, can shake both her left and right paws on command. This combination of tricks can be turned into a dance-in-place behavior called hot coals. When she is told, "Watch out for the hot coals," Yoli performs the shake left and shake right in sequence several times, which is quite entertaining to watch.

"high five," or whatever special word you have chosen for the behavior.

5. Slowly move your hand to the right so that your dog will turn his head to the left and track the treat. This motion will force the dog to go a bit off balance and take weight off his right front foot.

6. If he lifts that paw off the ground, even just a little, immediately open the hand and deliver the treat.

7. Repeat.

8. As the dog begins to raise his paw with greater enthusiasm, wait a bit longer before delivering the treat.

9. Hold out your left hand to receive his paw.

10. Eventually, eliminate the closed hand, relying on the verbal cue alone.

11. Reward the dog less frequently and on a random schedule.

12. Reverse the exercise, using a mirror image of the steps to teach your dog to shake with the other paw.

Shake Paw Method 2:
The Paw-Challenged Dog

Some dogs do not want to lift their feet off the ground, even if you use the method described above. These dogs need a little extra help understanding your expectations.

1. Begin with your dog sitting in front of you. If necessary, use a lead to keep him close.

2. Hold a high-value treat in your hand. Your dog should be able to see and reach it.

3. Present the treat at his nose level. You might even allow him to lick it to distract him.

4. In an upbeat tone of voice, give the command "shake."

5. Keeping the treat at his nose level, reach down with your other hand and gently tap the backside of his "wrist" between the upper pad and his foot. Use a tapping action like one you might use to test reflexes in a knee joint.

The shake paw is the root behavior behind the wave. You can morph the wave into a salute by rewarding a very high and stable outstretched paw.

6. *Immediately* reward even the slightest lift of the dog's foot.
7. Repeat.
8. Once the dog is presenting a raised foot, wait longer before delivering the treat to encourage a higher paw.
9. Present a hand for your dog to shake.
10. Eventually eliminate the touch on the wrist, relying on the verbal cue alone.
11. Reward him less frequently and on a random schedule.

> When using the Incentive Method, always reward approximations of the desired behavior rather than waiting for your dog to present the final version of the trick. As your dog starts to understand what you are seeking, wait longer to deliver the goodies.

The Wave

Any dog that has been taught to shake paw can be taught to wave. The wave is different from the shake paw in that:

- The paw is held higher.
- The paw is repeatedly waved up and down before being put back on the ground.
- The paw is not placed in your hand.
- The dog should be able to wave while you stand off at a distance.

To teach your dog to wave, first follow the instructions for shake paw. Then, once your dog is performing the shake paw reliably, widen your expectations. Step farther away and eliminate the added cue of presenting your hand to the dog.

To start this adaptation, pay attention to all the little cues associated with the shake

Cue Words

Most dogs understand that several words may mean the same thing. A case in point is a dog's name. It is not uncommon for a dog named Butch to recognize and respond to other names, such as Butchy Boy, Butch-o-Bob, Baba Butchie, and Love Dumpling Cutie Pie. In the same respect, many dogs adjust quite readily to new cue words for the same behavior, especially if most other things remain the same. Trick training often requires morphing one behavior into another. The wave, for instance, is a modified shake paw. To teach the new behavior, you add a new cue word to the already known behavior, then slowly add new expectations.

paw exercise. Note whether you lean forward, present your left or right hand, or use a unique tone of voice. While keeping those techniques constant, swap the word "wave" in place of "shake." Since most dogs pay more attention to our physical cues rather than our spoken words, your dog will more than likely perform a shake even when you say "wave." Praise and reward!

To achieve the wave, remember that in comparison to the shake:

1. The paw is held higher—so wait to praise and reward your dog until her foot is at its highest position. Hold the treat higher over her head.
2. The paw is repeatedly waved up and down before being put back on the ground—so wait to praise and reward until your dog raises her paw twice in a row, then three times, then more. Do not reward your dog if she puts her foot on the ground between waves.
3. The paw is not placed in your hand—so withdraw your outstretched hand a few

inches at a time until you are no longer presenting it. Exchange your outstretched hand with a waving hand signal.

4. The dog should be able to wave while you stand off at a distance—so slowly move farther and farther from your dog when giving the command. Remember to praise her immediately for the behavior, even if you cannot deliver the treat.

The Crawl

The crawl is a cute trick that can be used as part of a little skit. Imagine how funny it might be if you set up a bar jump that you tell an audience your dog will leap. You may go on and on about what a superb jumper your dog has become, bragging excessively about the athleticism of your super pup. Getting the audience involved by asking them to cheer on your agile canine, you utter your command to "jump!" in a proud voice. Instead of leaping over the bar, your dog drops to his belly and crawls under a very low obstacle. The audience comes alive with laughter. This is an example of being creative with your command words. Your dog doesn't know the human meaning behind words, only the behavior that you establish for each word. To your dog, "jump" might mean "creep along on your tummy." You could also establish a different word for jump (perhaps "over") and then show off his real jumping talent after your audience has had a good laugh.

A valuable precursor behavior to the crawl is the down. To teach your dog to crawl, you will want to use a very high-value treat.

1. Tell your dog to go down.
2. Holding a treat close to the floor and within the dog's reach, give the command word "crawl" (or whatever word you choose).
3. As your dog reaches for the treat, pull it away about 6 to 12 inches directly in front of her, keeping it in contact with the floor.

Crawl

Kayleigh taught her Samoyed to lie down using the Social Compliance Method. Snowbelle has a fast and reliable down, which is required in many tricks, including the crawl.

When teaching the "crawl" command, position the treat very close to the dog's nose.

The speed and distance that you move the treat are critical. The key to success will be to determine how quickly the treat can be pulled away from the dog before he loses interest.

4. If she moves even a slight distance toward the treat, give her a small bit of it. Then pull it forward a bit more.

5. Any movement your dog makes toward the treat should result in a little morsel as an enticement to move forward a bit more.

6. If your dog lifts up her elbows to move forward in a true crawl motion, give her instant and exuberant praise and a large piece of the high-value treat.

7. Ask for more and more forward movement before delivery of the treat, but do not be stingy in the beginning or your dog will not understand what you want from her.

8. As she crawls farther and farther before expecting the treat, begin to assume a different position relative to the dog so that she will not be dependent upon your position and the position of the treat on the ground in front of her.

Troubleshooting the Crawl

The most common problem dogs experience with the crawl is the desire to get up into a sit position to move forward to acquire a treat. If your dog has this problem, gently touch her shoulders with one hand and present the treat with the other hand. Do not smash her down to the ground or make the exercise unpleasant for her. Use a light bit of pressure when she begins to get up. At the same time, move the treat back directly in front of her mouth, so she can focus on your expectation that she reach for the treat.

Roll Over

Roll over is comprised of three parts. First, the dog must lie down. Next, he must roll onto his side. Finally, he must roll onto his back and over onto his other side. Not all dogs feel comfortable rolling onto their backs. Since it is just a trick for fun, if your dog is highly resistant to the idea, find another trick to work on. After your dog understands that you will lure him into different positions and reward him, he may be more apt to go along with the roll-over adventure. It is important to recognize that some dogs find it stressful to learn in an environment where they feel less than secure. If your dog fits into this category, make certain that you train him in a fairly distraction-free environment. Use a high-value treat for this skill.

1. Instruct your dog to lie down.
2. In the beginning it is helpful to manipulate her to rock on a hip if she has not already done so. To lure her into position, present the treat at her nose, then move it toward her hip. This will usually help a dog rock.
3. Give the command word "roll."
4. Hold the treat in front of your dog's face. Move it upward and back over the top of her head and to one side. As she follows it, she will roll onto her side.
5. Reward her while she is on her side. You may need to repeat the first part of the exercise a few times to help a reluctant dog feel comfortable rolling onto her side
6. Once she is comfortable rolling onto her side, use the command "roll over." Hold

Roll Over

The dog is first asked to lie down. Then the treat is moved from his nose to his shoulder to encourage the initial roll onto his side.

Sometimes the handler must guide the dog by gently supporting a front leg to steer him onto his back.

Give praise and a reward immediately once your dog rolls over onto his side.

the treat in front of her face and move it upward over her head and to the side as you did before. This time, continue the movement all the way over to the ground on the other side.

7. Her body should follow her head, and she should roll right over.

8. Reward her.

Since this is the Incentive Method, don't forget to reward even approximate versions of the final, desired act. Some dogs need a gentle touch or lift around the elbow to help them roll over to the other side. If you pair your command word with the behavior and reward sufficiently, you will eventually be able to stand up and say the command word without visual cues. There's really nothing cuter than a dog dropping to the ground and rolling over without her handler luring her with hand motion.

The Tunnel

1. Sit your dog at one end of the a tunnel. If necessary, engage the services of a partner to hold your dog there.

2. Move to the opposite end of the tunnel. Get down so that your dog can see your face from his position.

3. Reach in and present a treat for him, giving the "tunnel" command.

4. Be very patient. Do not force your dog through the tunnel.

5. If he is reluctant but makes a move to go into the tunnel, entice him to move a bit deeper into it by tossing the treat so that it is just out of his reach.

6. Repeat the exercise. Remain calm and patient until your dog commits to moving through the whole tunnel.

To make your own tunnel, cut the end off a plastic trash barrel. Secure the barrel with weights or make a stand out of PVC. A quick search of the Internet will yield dozens of sites that provide clear instructions on how to make your own inexpensive agility obstacles.

Tunnel

Begin with a very short tunnel—shorter than 10 feet. To make your own tunnel, cut the bottom off a plastic barrel and secure it with weighted bags of sand or a stand made out of PVC. A quick search on the Internet will yield dozens of sites that have details on making your own agility equipment.

Never force a dog into a tunnel. Instead, lure him in with a treat. Some dogs need more encouragement than others. Ask a helper to hold your dog at one end of a short tunnel. Get down on the other side, reach all the way into it, and hand deliver a treat to your dog as a reward for merely sticking his nose into the end.

The Teeter

The teeter and dog walk are obstacles found in agility. Each requires your dog to walk up and down a sloping plank around 12 inches wide. It is wise to begin on a board that is a few inches off the ground, perhaps sitting on 8-inch concrete blocks. Using a high-value treat, lure the dog onto and across the plank. Hold the food as close to the board as possible to keep your dog's attention on the task. Once your dog can walk across a low board, you can begin to add pitch. A teeter board is about 12 feet long. It will be 2 feet off the ground at the pivot point. If possible, begin the training with a teeter that is only 1 foot high at the pivot. If you are able to train only on a regulation-size teeter, you will need the assistance of a helper.

Lure your dog up the board while your assistant holds the teeter stable. Once you reach the pivot point, ask your helper to very slowly lower the board a bit at a time. Allow your dog to adjust her balance as the board is lowered. When it is about halfway down, ask your dog to walk on, then wait as your helper lowers the board to the ground, taking care not to allow it to bang or bounce. The helper must continue to hold the board down as your dog exits to prevent it from slapping your dog in the rear end.

Teeter

The teeter is commonly seen in agility competitions. It is referred to as a contact obstacle. A zone at the end of the board is painted a different color than the rest of the plank. To avoid a nonqualifying score, a dog must put at least one foot in the contact zone before jumping off. Teaching your dog to slow down or pause at the end of the board helps ensure he will make contact.

Keep the treat very close to the board to encourage your dog to keep her head down. Continue to move forward to avoid a stalling-out behavior that can cause a dog to jump off the board.

Allow your dog to feel the board pivot. Keep your hand in her collar to prevent her from jumping off the board, but do not hold the collar or lead tight. Your dog must be in control of her own body to learn to balance on her own.

Keeping the treat low to the plank will keep your dog's head down too. This will encourage her to walk all the way off the board rather than jumping off it. Jumping could both injure the dog and result in her missing the contact zone when she is moving more quickly.

A lured behavior, the bow is a fun trick to perform and keeps your dog limber.

The Bow

Imagine standing in the lounge of a rehab center. All eyes are on you and your dog. You have found great joy in visiting nursing homes and children's hospitals with your therapy dog, as you see how happy the folks are to pet your best friend and share stories about their own dog. Volunteering your time to see people smile makes all the time and effort you have taken in training your dog worthwhile. Imagine that you and your pup have just completed a little skit. Everyone is clapping and cheering. It's time for your bow.

1. Start with your dog standing directly in front of you.
2. Hold a treat at your dog's nose level.
3. Command him to "take a bow!"
4. Move the treat diagonally toward the ground between his front feet.
5. As he follows the lure, he should lower his front end.
6. Reward any behavior that approximates a bow.
7. Repeat and work toward a more pronounced bow each time.

If you used the luring method to teach your dog to lie down, you may need to gently support his belly with one hand. Some dogs very routinely perform a stretch that appears to be a bow. For example, if every time you let your dog out of his crate he bows, you can attempt to capture that behavior by using your bridge (click or voice) and rewarding him. Add a cue word ("bow") just before he begins to stretch, then reinforce the behavior with a treat.

Some owners expect their dogs to catch treats from a great distance too early in the training process. Begin by dropping a treat from 1 inch above your dog's mouth. Even then, some dogs will fail to open their mouths in time to catch the treat. Take time and move the treat away slowly.

Catch Food or Toys

When I raise a litter of working border collie puppies, I feel it is critical to provide plenty of early socialization. Between the sixth and seventh week, I teach the puppies to take food out of my fingers. It never ceases to amaze me that it is a skill that a puppy must learn, and most puppies need practice to accomplish what appears to be so natural an act in an adult dog.

The coordination between mouth and eyes must be developed. That is true even more so if you would like to teach your dog to catch treats as you toss them. There are benefits to having a dog that is accomplished at catching treats. First, you can get a treat to the dog sooner rather than later so that he need not come back to you to acquire his reward. That can leave him in position to continue to another step in a process. Second, you can teach a dog to focus on your face in exercises such as watch or front during a recall. Third, it's really a fun trick to have up your sleeve. Finally, a dog that develops good eye-mouth coordination with food can learn to catch objects such as toys more quickly.

Start with very small pieces of soft treats. If your dog misses the catch, you do not want him banged in the face with a big, hard biscuit.

149

1. Sit your dog directly in front of you.
2. Hold a treat just 1 inch above his nose.
3. Give the command word "catch" or whatever creative word you think up.
4. Drop the treat.
5. If he catches it, praise him profusely.
6. If he doesn't catch the treat, allow him to snatch it up off the floor the first time so that he realizes how good it is. After the first time, prevent him from getting to the treat before you pick it up off the floor.
7. Repeat several times with the treat just 1 inch or so above the dog's nose until you see him actively open his mouth in an attempt to grab the snack.
8. Once he is opening his mouth, you can move the treat farther away.
9. You can eventually begin to toss the treat toward him.

Once your dog associates the word "catch" with the act of grabbing something with his mouth, you can begin to toss other items, such as a ball or toy.

Circle Left and Circle Right

Circle left and right is a great way to keep your dog limber. However, care should be taken to avoid creating a compulsively spinning dog. Some members of the herding breeds can both excel at and become neurotic about spinning. Always teach a left and a right circle to avoid asymmetrical muscle development.

Start with your dog standing. Hold a treat in front of his nose. Slowly move it in an arc toward his shoulder. Any initial movement in the desired direction should be rewarded. Over time, withhold the treat until the dog has accomplished first a half circle and then a full circle. This is another trick that can be entertaining with cute command words, such as "Do a tornado" or "Show me a hurricane."

Go to Your Place

As a child I recall going to the circus. Inside a huge cage, the big cat tamer displayed his talent as a trainer with the lions and tigers. While it was impressive that the cats would follow his instructions to jump through a hoop or over each other, I was most impressed at how each lion, after performing a trick, would go back to its home base and sit like a dog.

Teaching your dog to go to his place has a very utilitarian purpose, but it is also a great way to manage more than one dog during a performance. Begin by determining where you would like your dog to go. A raised platform can be a great option, as it is highly identifiable for your dog. A blanket is another option. The middle of a hula hoop lying on the ground can also serve as a "place" and double as a prop for tricks. Your dog's kennel crate is a sensible option too. Since a raised platform is the most sophisticated example, it will be presented.

Circle

Circle left or circle right can be taught with a standard luring method.

If your dog is reluctant, increase the value of the treat. Keep the lure at his nose level to avoid enticing him to jump up for the food.

Moving the lure from the nose to the shoulder typically gets the dog moving. With a large dog, it can be a struggle to position the lure to keep him moving in a circle, especially if you are not terribly tall. But with time and patience, you can teach your dog this fun trick.

Look at the pleasure this young handler, Sydney, displays for her dog's performance. It is a joy to work with kids who are focused and dedicated to teaching their dogs both basic obedience and tricks.

CHAPTER 8

1. Choose a platform that is 6 to 8 inches high. You can raise it later.
2. Give the "go to your place" command.
3. Using a high-value treat, lure the dog onto the platform.
4. Praise and reward her.
5. Repeat several times.
6. Once the dog is jumping onto the platform with ease and reliability, add the expectation of "sit" or "down," and "stay." Refer to Chapters 5 and 6 to learn to reinforce a sit or a down with a solid stay.
7. Expect your dog to remain on the platform in the sit or down position for a few seconds, then reward her.
8. Extend the time on the platform as the dog demonstrates consistency.
9. Move farther and farther away from the platform before telling your dog to "go to your place," directing him with the verbal command, a hand signal that indicates the direction of the platform, and a strong, focused gaze.
10. With practice, you should be able to send your dog to her place from across a large room or even a soccer field.
11. Apply the rules for extinguishing the food reward found in discussions of the Incentive Method.

Jump over the Bar

If you have plans to move beyond novice obedience trials or would like to show in agility trials, your dog will need to jump over things on command, sometimes carrying a dumbbell in his mouth.

The best method for introducing jumping is, of course, the Incentive Method. But a solid sit, which was taught using the Comprehensive Method, may be helpful in very early training. For the most control over the exercise, ask your dog to sit or stand on one side of a very low jump.

1. Step over the jump yourself to encourage a jump rather than a walk around.
2. Show your dog the treat.
3. Tap the top of the jump with your finger. This is the beginning of a directed hand signal.
4. Give your command to jump. (Remember, be creative with your commands.)
5. Step backward and lure your dog over the jump.
6. Praise and reward him.
7. Repeat.

Some agility handlers believe it is not prudent to teach your dog to jump directly at you. They prefer to teach dogs to move

Taking Care of Your Dog's Bones

Care should be taken to avoid demanding a young dog to perform repetitive actions that could put stress on his growing skeleton. Many people advise waiting until a dog's growth plates have closed prior to adding jumping to his training regimen. The growth plates are located at the ends of long bones, such as the femur. A dog's sex hormones, in conjunction with other hormone-related processes, initiate closure of the growth plates. Therefore, it is often suggested to avoid jumping until your dog has gone through puberty. Dogs that have been spayed prior to puberty may require additional time to mature before jumping. During early jumping, the height should be set very low, perhaps no higher than 8 inches for most dogs.

off and away from the handler to scout out and perform a jump just as the dog would be expected during a competition. However, since dogs are quite plastic in their ability to learn new things, and because your dog is least likely to fail or make a mistake when the exercise is well contained and clear, I recommend the following method to provide the basic connection between the cue word and the behavior.

Once your dog understands that you want him to jump on command, move to a position on the same side of the jump as he is.

1. Walk to the jump and point to it with your hand.
2. If it is wide enough, step over it while commanding your dog to jump. You will go over the jump with your dog.
3. Praise and reward him.
4. Once he understands what is expected of him when you are walking over the jump with him, approach the jump the same way as described above. But this time, step to one side and go around the outside of the jump while commanding him to jump.
5. Take your dog off lead.
6. Trot alongside your dog.
7. As you approach the jump, signal to it with your hand and command your dog to jump.
8. Wait until you and the dog are a few yards from the jump before offering a reward.

Jump over the Bar

Many trainers set the bar too high in early training. A dog that tips the bar with his foot and allows it to drop can experience a setback due to anxiety or fear. While dogs can overcome these issues, it's best to avoid them by using smart and conservative techniques.

Jump through the Hoop

Apply the steps found in jumping over a bar but substitute a hula hoop for the bar. Eliminate the step in which you move over the obstacle yourself. If necessary, make a frame to hold the hoop, or have a friend hold it during the early stages of training. Once your dog understands the concept, you can take over holding the hoop, raising it slowly in small increments and moving its position to create fun tricks.

Jump through the Hoop

Kids in a 4-H class help each other train their dogs.

159

Once your dog has mastered jumping through a hula hoop, you can teach him to jump through your arms! When he is reliably leaping through a stationary hoop (or an Agility tire jump), stand next to the hoop with an outstretched arm positioned just below the hoop. As he gains confidence performing that skill, add your other arm above the hoop. Finally, link your hands to form a circle around the hoop. Removing the hoop from the picture will be simple if you progress slowly. Do not increase the difficulty until your dog is performing each new step with greater than 80 percent reliability. *Juniors Bildarchiv/Photolibrary*

Dance

This trick can evolve out of the sit up exercise.

1. Give your dance command.
2. Hold a treat centered and slightly above your dog's head.
3. Raise it high enough that she cannot reach it without lifting at least one front foot off the floor.
4. Use the treat to lure your dog to stand on her back feet.
5. Praise and reward her for approximations of the final version, then finally only for standing on her back legs.
6. Once she is comfortable standing on her back legs, begin luring her to move in a circle to create the dance.

Note that some dogs are not physically capable of remaining on their back feet for very long. Never force a dog to perform a trick that seems to be physically uncomfortable.

Perry shows off his ability to "dance," which is taught using a luring method.

Sit Up

1. Start with your dog in a sit position.
2. Tell your dog to "sit pretty."
3. Hold a treat close to her chest.
4. Move the treat upward, past her nose and then above her head.
5. In the beginning, reward any attempt on her part to raise one or both of her front feet off the ground.
6. Hold off rewarding her until she begins to sit higher on her haunches.

Sit Up

The "sit pretty" command isn't just a cute trick. It can also provide exercise for your dog's core muscles and help him develop better balance.

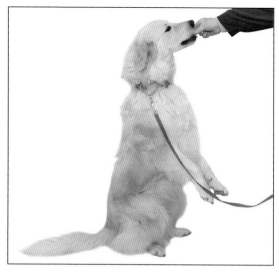

If you plan to work your dog in agility, tricks such as sit pretty may offer benefits well beyond the cuteness factor.

Once your dog is able to assume the position, expect him to hold it a bit longer each day. This work can strengthen his balance.

TEACHING USEFUL SKILLS

There are behaviors that, while taught as tricks, may become very useful skills. In this chapter, behaviors that are typically on the list of tasks performed by service dogs will be presented. First introduced as tricks, the standards for the behaviors may be set at a very high level using the Comprehensive Method. When a person

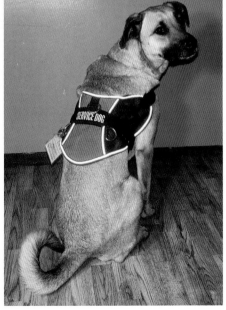

Bree is a service dog in training. Through the Incentive Method, she learned many tricks that were then transferred to valuable tasks she can perform for a disabled person. To travel in public with her partner, Bree must demonstrate exceptional social skills. She must comply with basic obedience commands at a very high level to maintain her status as a functioning service dog.

with a disability asks her dog to perform a duty, the dog mustn't think that it is simply a game in which the dog may choose to participate. While learning the tricks that are presented in this chapter, keep in mind that any behavior, if the handler finds necessary, could be turned into a compulsory command simply by using the Comprehensive Method once the dog has learned the task.

Push Shut with Nose

Refer to Chapter 3 and teach your dog to touch a target with his nose. The target can be a small paper plate or a plastic yogurt lid. Once your dog is touching the target reliably, you can move the target to a cabinet. Adhere it to the door with a bit of tape. Over time, you can exchange the word "touch" with "push shut." Do not add too much novelty at the same time, so refrain from taping the target onto the door and changing the cue word on the same day. If your dog struggles with understanding a new cue word, say the original cue "touch" directly before the new words "push shut." Then eliminate the cue "touch." Your dog will learn to push shut the door with his nose.

Depending upon your situation, you may want to give each cabinet a different name (the cabinet in the kitchen versus the cabinet in the bathroom, for example). Or you may rely on your dog's ability to follow the direction of your gaze or the direction in which you point and use the same command word for all the doors you want him to push shut. The better you identify the target to be pushed shut, the easier it will be for your dog to learn the task.

As with all incentive-based skills, remember to reward approximate behaviors early on, then expect a more highly refined version of the final task as your dog becomes accomplished and confident with your expectations.

Close It with Paw

Refer to Chapter 8 to teach the basic "shake paw" command. Once your dog can perform a reliable shake paw, you can transfer that skill to a variety of other useful tasks.

First, teach your dog to shake with a target of some sort. Instead of receiving his paw into your hand, hold a small paper plate or plastic lid in your hand and give the command to shake. When your dog presents his paw and touches the target, praise him profusely and reward him.

In time, move the target from the palm of your hand to a position slightly to the left or right of where you would normally present your hand for a shake. Work toward your dog reaching for the target with his paw. Remember to reward approximate attempts in the beginning. Your dog should eventually be able to touch the target regardless of where you place it. At that time, you can attach it to an open cabinet door.

Over time, transfer the command word "shake" to "close it." The same rules apply about transferring the command word and eliminating the target as in the above exercise to "push shut." Dogs quickly learn to focus where you focus. Gaze upon the door you want your dog to close. It will provide more information than you might imagine.

Turn off Light with Paw

When your dog has learned to shake paw with a target on a cabinet door in order to close it, it's time to move the target to a wall. Begin with the target at a level that is very easy for your dog to reach with his paw. When he is reliably touching the target on the wall, replace it with a light switch plate. Introduce a new cue word. Gradually move the light switch plate up the wall until it is at the height of a normal light switch. Once the dog is working on the actual light switch, begin to reward only those times when his paw actually

While having a dog that can fetch a beer during the Super Bowl may be awe inspiring, be careful what you wish for. A dog that has been trained to pull open the refrigerator door and fetch a can of soda might also find the cheese or leftover lasagna irresistible when you go off to work. A good game of tug is the basis for the "pull open" command.

strikes the switch and makes the light turn on or off. Reward him profusely for each new accomplishment along the way.

Pull Open

One method I have avoided presenting up to now is encouragement through play. Dogs present many behaviors during play sessions. Many of them can become useful skills if attached to commands. However, capturing these skills can be somewhat haphazard, unless you have exceptional timing and are quite skilled at marking behaviors with a bridge.

Many dogs enjoy a good game of tug-of-war. If your dog is one of them, you are well on your way to teaching her to pull on command. Encourage your dog to tug on a piece of rope by playing with a toy that contains a rope. Use the command "tug" or "pull" when the dog clamps down on the object and will tolerate your pulling back a bit. This is a game of tug-of-war that you will win. Not all dogs will play this game. I have found that dogs that are highly respectful of humans may not think tug-of-war is an appropriate diversion. For those dogs, see "The Tug-Challenged Dog" section on the next page.

Once the dog is showing great enthusiasm for the tug-of-war game with a rope, you can attach a small piece of rope to a cabinet door. Early on, do not expect the dog to pull past the magnetic or mechanical hinging mechanism. Instead, leave the door slightly ajar to make pulling easy. Tell the dog to pull, and touch or point to the pull rope. In the beginning, reward even the slightest attempt to make contact with the rope.

Pull Shut a Full-Size Door

As the dog gains more confidence in pulling, put a size-appropriate tug rope on a full-size door, the refrigerator door, or any other hinged object. You may give each door a unique cue word or simply point to the tug rope and say "pull shut."

Pull a Box or Container

If a lead or other rope is attached to a wheeled container (or flat bottom box on a smooth surface), such as an egg crate or small-sized, lightweight child's wagon, you can teach your dog to pull it with his mouth. Begin by requesting him to tug a toy attached to the handle of the container. Praise and reward him for very small movements, then expect more distance.

The Tug-Challenged Dog

Some dogs do not play tug-of-war very well. These are often meek dogs that have a very natural reverence for human authority. They can still learn to pull open a door but cannot be encouraged through the tug game. First teach the dog to take and hold a rope toy (see Chapter 7). Replace the command words "take it" with "tug it." Move to the stage in training where the dog will take the toy from the surface of a counter or tabletop rather than directly from your hands. When the dog is reliably taking the toy off the table, add a bit of weight to the toy by securing it under the corner of a big book. This will create some resistance and require a stronger tug. Don't be surprised if the dog drops the rope and loses interest with the added resistance. Remain patient. Slowly adjust the amount of resistance required for the dog to "tug it" until he is required to put some decent force into the tug. Eventually, transfer the rope to the knob of a cabinet and instruct the dog pull the door open using the "tug" command.

Pull Clothes out of Dryer

This task combines a standard retrieve with the ability to handle cloth objects. It can be challenging for some dogs to place their heads into closed areas, such as clothes dryers. Select a cloth object and follow the instructions for retrieving in Chapter 7. Once your dog can perform a reliable retrieve, move the piece of clothing to the dryer door, first draping it on the opening, then putting it into the dryer. Make certain that the dryer and its contents are not hot.

While typically considered work that a service dog might perform for a person with a disability, taking clothes out of the dryer is a fun task that you can train your dog to do. Most dogs feel fulfilled when they have an important job to do. A fulfilled dog is less likely to act out in frustration and destroy property.

Put Clothes in Basket or Put an Object on the Counter

In Chapter 7, we described the retrieve in great detail. The instructions explain how to teach a dog to deliver an object to your hand. There might be times when you would like your dog to put an object somewhere else rather than bringing it to you.

Once the dog is highly confident with retrieving, you can morph the "give" command (which is "to hand") into a "drop it in" or "put in on" skill.

1. Place a box directly next to you.
2. Ask your dog to fetch an item.
3. When he brings it back, instead of saying "give," point to the box and say "give, drop it." Allow the object to fall through your hands into the box.
4. Praise and reward your dog profusely. The dog that was taught to hold and not drop an object, and that was asked to pick it back up if he did accidentally drop it,

needs quick feedback to learn that you are happy that he has dropped the item (even though, in his mind, you failed to catch it when he handed it over).
5. Repeat.
6. Slowly move the box farther and farther away. Remember to look at and point to the box in the beginning.
7. Eliminate the "give" part of the command after the dog has successfully accomplished the task a few times.

To teach your dog to place an object onto a surface rather than in a container, follow a similar process. Stand next to a table that is at your dog's chin level. Follow the steps above but ask the dog to "give, put it here." Point to the top of the table, hold your hands over the table, and allow the object to slide from your hands to the tabletop. Praise your dog profusely. Eliminate the "give" part of the command once the dog has been successful a few times.

Having taken clothes from the dryer, Bree assists her partner by dropping them into a basket. Unfortunately, Bree does not know how to fold or iron, and she doesn't do windows. But her services are invaluable to her disabled partner, who gains increased independence through the jobs Bree performs.

Chapter 10

Conclusion

I t was a very cold, damp, and dark November evening. I had traveled the 70 miles home from my job in corporate America through pouring rain and I was tired. As I pulled up the drive at my little farm in rural Wisconsin, I saw that the sheep were standing in the far pasture. They were vulnerable in what I had come to refer to as coyote darkness. First on the list of chores was to bring them into the barn and lock them up for their safety. I dreaded having to go out in the frigid sleet, but at least I had my trusted dog Sham to do most of the work.

A quick change out of my dress clothes and off we went, my loyal dog and I. Sham was my first border collie and the reason I even had a farm with sheep. The details of how he came to be my dog are a story in themselves. Suffice it to say that from a third-floor apartment in Chicago, I had traveled two hours to take my first herding lesson just a few years earlier. I won my first herding trial with Sham a few months thereafter. I purchased for him his own sheep before I had my own real estate on which to maintain them, keeping them on a friend's farm for enough months to outstay my welcome. That day in November, he was serving me in the capacity of his genetic heritage, and I was certain it would be a quick job to get the sheep into the barn so I could get out of the weather.

While the cold rain pelted me, I stood by the gate waiting. I had sent Sham to gather his charges, and it was just a matter of time for the sheep to make their way to the barn, where I would shut them in for the night. It was an activity that we performed several

times a week—any time the sheep had not found their way to the barn by themselves before my arrival home from work. But instead of moving right past me and through the familiar passage, the sheep stalled at the gate opening. Sham stood his ground, preventing any individuals from turning back. Frustrated by the lack of progress, I began giving him commands. He stood his ground, refusing my instructions. I suppose it was the weather and fatigue that got the best of me, but I finally lost my cool. At the top of my lungs, I bellowed a flank command, with searing disapproval of my dog's apparent disregard for my authority.

In response and without moving a muscle, Sham flashed the white of his eyes in my direction, then went back to eyeing his ewes. It was a look I will never forget. While it occurred in less than a second, the meaning behind the gaze was immensely apparent. Had he been able to speak English, I truly believe that Sham would have said to me, "Are you bloody out of your mind, woman?" Obviously, Sham knew how to work sheep. and he realized that if he were to comply with my commands, the results would be utterly disastrous. It was an intense moment. I knew that my next move was central to both the success of the mission and the maintenance of our relationship. I exhaled and chose to relinquish control of the situation to my dog. I relaxed and shut up. Within twenty seconds, with just a tip of his ear to the left and a little baby step to the right, Sham convinced his sheep to move forward and they filed into the barn with great composure.

This book has focused on teaching you how to take responsibility for your dog's social well-being. It has provided methods to help your dog become a well-adjusted, compliant, respectful, happy member of your family. It has included instruction on fun tricks and useful skills that, when taught properly, will enhance the bond you have with your dog. But one last message must be included. Perhaps it is the most important message you can take away from this tome.

The flow of information for nearly all the exercises presented in this book has been from you as teacher to your dog, the student. However, the lessons you can learn from your dog may be more profound and enriching than any skill you teach your pup. Because I had trained Sham with appropriate methods that were designed to develop our relationship, there came times when he became my greatest teacher. Surrendering control to a dog is a humbling experience. It can be successful only when the trust and

reverence is mutual. The value in cultivating a respectful relationship with your dog is that you can at times give him the helm and he will not take advantage of the authority you grant to him. It is at those times when the connection between human and beast is its richest and most intense.

While I am not one to often complain that life isn't fair, the mismatch of life span between canine and human is one of the greatest injustices in nature. Sham's existence in my life was so pivotal and enriching that it seems like just yesterday when he taught me both sophisticated and simple lessons about how to be a better person. Yet it has been more than a decade since I last stroked his soft fur and told him "that'll do" after a job well done. The final lesson I wish to impart in this book is to remind you to cherish each day you have with your dog and make it the best experience for both of you. While your dog will one day become just a fond memory, the lessons he can teach you, if you so permit, will last a lifetime.

DarnFar Boon is a grandson of Sham, the author's first border collie. Although they were big shoes to fill, Boon has taken over the role of partner and loyal companion, tasks that were once assigned to his magnificent grandfather.

RESOURCES

4-H Resources
National 4-H Council
7100 Connecticut Avenue
Chevy Chase, MD 20815
phone: 301-961-2800
website: http://4-h.org/

National 4-H Headquarters
1400 Independence Ave., S.W., Stop 2225
Washington, DC 20250-2225
website: http://www.national
4-hheadquarters.gov/

National Organizations that Offer All Breed Trials in Obedience, Agility, Rally, or Other Competitions
American Kennel Club
website: www.akc.org

AKC Companion Events Obedience
Regulations
Obedience, Agility, and Tracking Number:
(919) 816-3557
phone: (919) 816-3521
fax: (919) 816-4204
email: obedience@akc.org

AKC Agility Regulations
phone: (919) 816-3725, (919) 816-3509
Jump Height Cards: (919) 816-3821
fax: (919) 816-4204
email: agility@akc.org

AKC Rally Regulations
phone: (919) 816-3521

fax: (919) 816-4204
email: rally@akc.org

AKC Tracking (scent work) Regulations
phone: (919) 816-3521
fax: (919) 816-4204
email: tracking@akc.org

AKC Public Education
phone: (919) 816-3712
fax: (919) 816-4275

AKC Canine Good Citizen
phone: (919) 816-3637
fax: (919) 816-4203
email: cgc@akc.org

Australian Shepherd Club of America (ASCA)
Despite its name, ASCA allows all breeds and
mixed breeds into its nonconformation events
6091 E. State Hwy 21
Bryan, TX 77808-9652
phone: (979) 778-1082
fax: (979) 778-1898
email: activities@asca.org
website: http://www.asca.org/

Canine Performance Events (CPE)
P.O. Box 805
South Lyon, MI 48178
email: cpe@charter.net
website: http://www.k9cpe.com/

North American Dog Agility Association
North American Dog Agility Council
(NADAC)

P.O. Box 1206
Colbert, OK 74733
email: info@nadac.com
website: http://www.nadac.com/

Mixed Breed Dog Clubs of America
(MBDCA)
c/o Linda Lewis, Membership Secretary
13884 State Route 104
Lucasville, OH 45648-8586
phone: (740)-259-3941
email: Libi-Lew@juno.com
website: http://www.mbdca.org/

United Kennel Club (UKC)
100 E. Kilgore Rd.
Kalamazoo MI 49002-5584
phone: 269-343-9020
fax: 269-343-7037
website: http://www.ukcdogs.com/

United States Dog Agility Association
P.O. Box 850955
Richardson, TX 75085-0955
phone: 972-487-2200 Ext. 102
email: info@usdaa.com
website: http://www.usdaa.com/

National Organizations that Offer Therapy Dog Certification

The Delta Society
875 124th Ave. NE, Ste. 101
Bellevue, WA 98005
phone: (425) 679-5500
fax: (425) 679-5539
email: info@deltasociety.org
website: http://www.deltasociety.org

Therapy Dogs Inc.
P.O. Box 20227
Cheyenne, WY 82003
email: therapydogsinc@qwestoffice.net
phone: 877-843-7364
phone: 307-432-0272
fax: 307-638-2079
website: http://www.therapydogs.com/

Therapy Dogs International
88 Bartley Road
Flanders, NJ 07836
phone: (973) 252-9800
fax: (973) 252-7171
email: tdi@gti.net
website: www.tdi-dog.org

Interesting Dog-related Websites

Animal World's Dog Page
http://animal-world.com/dogs/

DarnFar Ranch: The Author's Website
http://www.darnfar.com

Dog Play: Activities For Dogs
http://www.dogplay.com/

InfoDog
http://www.infodog.com/

The FBI's Page about Dogs: For Kids
http://www.fbi.gov/kids/dogs/doghome.htm

The Dog Channel
http://www.dogchannel.com/

The Dog Help Site
http://www.doghelpsite.com

Companies that Specialize in Dog Obedience Supplies

All K-9
http://www.allk-9.com/

Fetch Dog
http://www.fetchdog.com/Shop

J & J
http://www.jjdog.com/

Max200
http://www.max200.com/

The Leash Connection
http://www.dog-training.com/

Things 4 Your Dog
http://www.things4yourdog.com/

Working Dogs Outfitter
http://www.workingdogs.com/

Large Dog Supply Companies: Specializing in Wholesale Prices to the Public

Discount Pet Supply Store
http://www.discount-pet-superstore.com/

Dog.com
www.dog.com

Gun Dog Supply
http://www.gundogsupply.com/

Pet Edge
www.petedge.com

Companies that Specialize in or Offer Therapy Dog and Service Dog Products

Active Dogs
http://www.activedogs.com/

Pet Joy
http://www.petjoyonline.com/

Service Dog Supplies Unlimited
http://www.servicedogsuppliesunlimited.com/

Sit Stay
http://www.sitstay.com

Two Tuttles
http://www.servicedoghouse.com/

Wolf Packs
http://wolfpacks.com/products/servicedog/

INDEX

ABOUT THE AUTHOR

Tammie Rogers and her husband Robert, reside in Brownstown, Illinois, where they operate DarnFar Ranch, a full-service, professional dog training facility. Assisted by border collies, they also maintain a commercial flock of Dorper-cross sheep. Tammie provides instruction in basic through advanced obedience, service dog training, and livestock herding, as well as teaching the 4-H dog training classes. Several of her students have earned high honors at the state fair. In 2002, Tammie left a 20-year career as a biologist in the biomedical field to devote her full attention to dogs and their people.